Painterly Painting

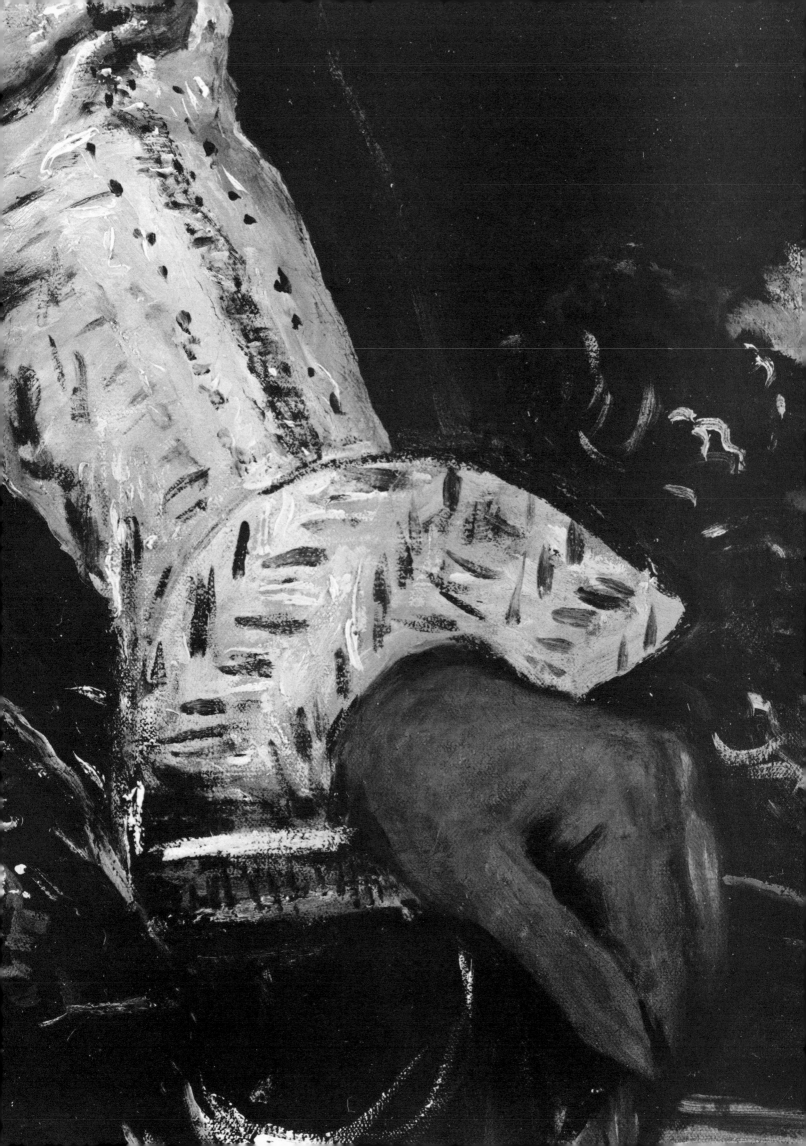

Art News Annual XXXVII

Painterly Painting

Edited by Thomas B. Hess and John Ashbery

The Macmillan Company, New York

Left: Air, matter, space, light defined in the strokes of a
painterly style: Detail of Velazquez' *Philip IV of Spain
in Brown and Silver*, ca. 1630. National Gallery, London.

Cover: Titian's famous late work, *The Rape of Europa* (detail),
1562, in the series of mythological fables he painted
for Philip II. Isabella Stewart Gardner Museum, Boston.

Art News Annual (incorporating Portfolio)
is published each October by Newsweek, Inc.
444 Madison Avenue, New York, N.Y. 10022

Art News Annual is distributed for
Newsweek, Inc. by The Macmillan Company,
866 Third Avenue, New York, N.Y. 10022

Contents

9   Thoughts about Painterly: By Louis Finkelstein

25   Roman Illusionism: By Sheldon Nodelman

39   The Great Venetians: By Terisio Pignatti

57   The Sketch: By E. Haverkamp-Begemann

75   Fragonard: By Francis Watson

89   Constable: By Rodrigo Moynihan

105   Hans Hofmann: By Elizabeth C. Baker

117   Willem de Kooning: By John Ashbery

129   Painterly vs. Painted: By Carter Ratcliff

148   Index

150   Advertisements

Managing Editor	Elizabeth C. Baker
Executive Editor	Harris Rosenstein
Senior Editor	Henry A. La Farge
Associate Editor	Dolores Fenn
Editorial Associate	Joyce Clarke
Design Director	Bradbury Thompson
Production Manager	Angelo Cutro
Production Assistant	Robert Preato
Publisher	Alvin Garfin
Assistant to the Publisher	Warren Kask
Advertising Sales	Sephine B. Melrod, Marian Conner
Advertising Assistant	Patricia A. Kehoe

By Louis Finkelstein

Thoughts about Painterly

Its poetry is at the same time formal, descriptive, psychological, metaphysical

Painter Louis Finkelstein spent 1970-71, his
sabbatical year, away from a professorship at Queens
College, New York, in Aix-en-Provence, from where
he renewed his acquaintanceship with European museums,
worked in Cézanne's countryside and wrote this essay.

Thoughts about Painterly

Painterly—a kind of slop or a kind of sloppiness; whether as a habit of mind or as a set of physical characteristics.

Also, the way in which a painting was good. Like the dealer who said (albeit some time ago): "If it's Abstract-Expressionist we know it's good." Sometime in the 1950s I came back from being away a while in Europe and a painter I knew spoke to me about something he called "New York paint." I was shocked at the idea that there was a certain kind of paint *of* New York. Later, of course, the same paint was seen in places like Warsaw, Rome, Tokyo and the University of California. Later it was replaced by acrylics.

Also the way a painting was bad. Like in Post-Painterly which meant you were supposed to have outgrown all that. This frequently had the smell of Great Renunciations, like all the people who never learned to draw in the first place giving up Nature. But this was no worse than the people who discovered that they *were* Nature and therefore didn't have to learn to draw.

Originally, in Wölfflin's usage, painterly was an art historical classificatory device which in his exposition carried with it the implication that in at least certain of its manifestations it was the working out of a kind of logic of historical development. Past a certain point in time, however, it may be that the distinction has a different character and a different historical implication, more than anything else like the resistance to strict historical determination.

At a certain point painterly signified a kind of Dutch courage, which was, of course, originally an epithet for gin, but in this case was the courage of a particular Dutchman, namely de Kooning, as if you could put on his paint in the same way you could put on his clothes if you borrowed them or stole them.

Most of the difficulties with painterly stem from this borrowed clothes idea, otherwise the fallacy of misplaced concreteness, which is the mistaking of the nature of a thing for a few of its attributes.

In the case of painterly, the misplaced concreteness springs from four sources, but since everybody knows

that real explanations are in threes, we will have to reduce the number by one. This is easy because one of the explanations is when the term is used as part of a sales pitch, as in "Abstract-Expressionism is Good"; since in the long run (in the language of Ogden and Richards' *The Meaning of Meaning*, this comes out as that to which the user of a symbol would like to have somebody else believe he is referring) all words can be used in sales pitches, the distinction is neither here nor there and so we are back to three:

1. From the propensity of art historians to collect things on "objective" bases. This may help settle some of their problems, but it doesn't seem to help anyone else.

2. From the simplistic esthetics which holds that the basis of art is the unity of formal relations among our sense perceptions. This is properly referred to as a formalist position in spite of some people's objection to the term. It is sometimes disguised as the assertion that the only statements which can be made intelligibly about works of art are in terms of such unities; there is here enshrined a confusion as between intelligibility and adequacy as principles of explanation.

3. From the simplistic estimates of the nature of perception which explain it on the level of sense impressions, the elements of the retinal image, such as color and shape. Pedagogically such estimates are found from Ruskin's teaching of drawing all the way down to Bauhaus-inspired "design" or "visual fundamentals" courses which propose that they will teach people "how to see."

"Style" for the artist means something different than it does for the art historian. The claim by the latter that by standing aside from the particular confusions typical of the activity of the former he is somehow above the battle has the same cogency as the claims of military historians which Tolstoy derides as bestowing on events a greater degree of clarity than the events warrant.

For the historian, "style" is the constancy or regular change through time of tabulatable characteristics, including those of which the artist may not himself be aware. Whatever may be the attractions of this statistical approach it has the effect of making of the artist a layman, i.e. of denying a particularity to those functions *as artist,* and of making him then a kind of laborer in certain materials. (Given the recent expansion of the kinds of materials in vogue, this might have to be recast to a kind of laborer whose output is merchandized at certain kinds of outlets or under certain auspices.)

For the artist on the other hand, "style" represents the closure of a set of symbolizing or symbol-forming intentions. In the formative stages of a style, the painting elements are at the same time discrete technical solutions and glimmerings of possible meanings. Seeing further into the meanings provides the basis for relatively novel technical solutions. Such processes have a dual effect: one facing inward to the individual work where the possible efficacy of certain ways of symbolizing is tested by the kind of unification or corroboration of meaning which takes place in a given confluence, the other facing outward in the sense of expanding an available shared vocabulary. So that what was at issue in Gorky looking at Matta and saying, "Oh, thin paint,"

was not simply the picking up of a recipe (the borrowed clothes), so much as a revision of his understanding of the strategy of imaging, and consequently an uprooting and revaluation of all his modes of feeling, these being transvalued by their connection to new concrete terms.

That the transaction occurs on grounds of symbolizing (i.e., being tested by its meaning) rather than on "structural" grounds makes all the difference. There is no grammar of painting, but rather a plurality of rhetorics.

Painterly both is and is not one thing, is and is not transmissible.

Between technique, vision, intention, design, expression there is no seam; neither is one thing the cause and another the result.

Velazquez: *Portrait of Philip IV* as a young king, ca. 1626-28. Prado Museum, Madrid.

Velazquez: *Portrait of Philip IV*, ca. 1655-60. National Gallery, London.

The liquid touch in Rubens' late works astonished his contemporaries:
The Garden of Love (detail), ca. 1632. Prado, Madrid.

Renoir and the joy of painting: *Sunset at Sea*,
1883, 18 inches high. Clark Art Institute, Williamstown.

Learning is not a bad thing either. Sometimes learning is represented as either not necessary or, more subtly, as to be taken for granted. That is, it is assumed that the artist possesses as much learning as he needs and that this is self-evident. Robert Goldwater has pointed out that this fallacy derives from Riegl's formulation of "will-to-form," which assumes the adequacy of technique. It is much more the case that the artist does what he does because he literally doesn't know (how to do) any better. But the separation of learning and intention is artificial. I am willing to take it à la Riegl, provided that the proposition is seen as a two-way street, i.e. that artists with rudimentary techniques are stupid in the sense that the undeveloped nature of their technical concerns prevents them from having a very developed will to form, indeed is a sanctification of their ignorance. I think there is much to confirm this view. Conceptual Art is, after all, mostly a matter of willingness to be satisfied with what(ever) one does.

One of the particular fascinations of the Prado is that it shows several cycles of learning, the works that painters learned from and the works which show what was learned. We see both the genealogy and the elaboration of an idea. Most particularly painterly.

That painterly idea we might represent to be the subordination of individual objects to the sense of the circumambient medium, or the rendering of optical values as distinct from tactile, or as giving weight through color rather than through modeling, or as a distinction of focus through variations of brushstroke, etc. Yet as clear and available as these notions are, they do not succeed in obviating the necessity for each artist to work it out for himself. In spite of the relations between the styles of Titian, Rubens, Velazquez, Goya, each painterly style is unmistakably the result of individual idiosyncratic development. Indeed the artist does not appear deliberately to create the painterly style which is eventually his. Rather it is the result or realization of several successive kinds of reading into the way paint symbolizes air, matter, space, light, flesh. Anything we should call a formal structure is a by-product. Successive insights or projections of meaning take place like the cartoon idea of a lightbulb going on in one's head, each one click, discrete from what had gone before, supported by it yet novel, essentially about the meaning of paint. The same artist at different stages sees different meanings. Titian, when he begins to twist and bend the voluptuous flesh and satin of his holy figures so that they swell and catch the light at different angles did not foresee that deep and rich and shimmering soup where all drawing disappears and bulk expands into the encircling void as in the late Entombments. Rubens, in *The Garden of Love* (or *Feast of Venus*), makes of paint an entirely different substance than in other of his works, a transformation of which his closest collaborators had not an inkling. Velazquez, in a late study of Philip as against when Philip was a young man is engaged in an entirely different projective activity as to the nature not only of paint but of flesh, bone, head, etc., which belies completely the stereotype of his "dispassionate objectivity."

In Rembrandt's *Self-Portrait* in Washington, the almost microscopic irregularities of the paint surface fade in and out of focus on the quality of fleshiness in a manner defying calculation and owing nothing at all to the whole entire remainder of the language of chiaroscuro painting whether in Rembrandt's work or elsewhere.

In a similar fashion in the work of middle Renoir to late Renoir, middle Monet to late Monet, the grounds of translation are completely changed. In and out of the work of Renoir with no apparent rule there is the occurrence of monumental weightiness to forms, and these could be of figures, landscape or even still-life, produced by the sudden access of particular stridencies of color contrast.

In virtually every case, painterly seems an inherently, in principle, particularistic phenomenon, which receives new light or new definition of the meaning of means in terms of each instance, the important common feature

Early Monet: *Portrait of Jean Monet*, 1871, 16 inches high. Private collection.

Late Monet: *Nymphéas*, 1908. Durand-Ruel, Paris.

One kind of bravura: Manet's
Mme. Jean Martin in Black Hat, pastel, 1881.

Another kind of bravura: Boldini's *Mme. Marthe Letellier*,
ca. 1890. Private collection.

being the kind of projective activity which is involved both for the painter and the viewer.

As for example when you first look at the *Syndics of the Cloth Guild* it seems as if all the figures are in a row (which is also the way Rivers paints it) and then you see that the space is actually deeper than it is wide, which changes light, gesture, characterization, all.

Such senses of discovery (which are of an altogether different nature than iconographic discovery and invoke an altogether different order of transformation) could not, it would seem, occur without a certain amount of what appears to be slop, since they move from the known to the unknown to the known, unpredictably and unheralded.

Painterly can be, of course, a sort of indulgence, even self-indulgence, as, for example, when the bravura brushstroke provides a permission to insulate oneself from the demand of investigating further the symbolizing of experiences, that is when it stops short, when the meaning is limited *in an arbitrary way*. What constitutes arbitrary is a judgment which each observer must make for himself, and in so doing, pay for, in the sense of then permitting his own estimates of truth and value to be formed by the acceptance of that level of resolution (or not resolution.)

It would be unkind to point a finger; everyone succumbs to this to a degree. To return to the Prado for

a moment, the ultimate dimension of what is learned, one painter from another, is just this sustaining of penetration so that the artist continually moves past a simply available solution to one which has greater depth. The high level of demand is the result of a high level of competition.

Painterly can consist simply in being charmed with one's own paint. I think this is what is involved in a comparison between Boldini and Manet; although it becomes apparent that Manet's paint simply as paint is actually better, it is on some other level of awareness that this takes place so that we do not say that he is charmed by it. This distinction may be no distinction, however, because at a certain moment one (whether it is the spectator or the artist himself would be irrelevant here) may be charmed and then at a later moment see into it, that is beyond the merely charming, although that particular charm might remain as the talisman for a deeper dimension. Philip Guston, it seems, has had a particularly bad time of it, having been attacked from all sides on this score. When his "painterly" works were first shown in the early 1950s he was charged with being charmed with his own paint (this was of course at a certain time considered reprehensible), then later of abandoning the sensuous quality of his earlier work, then later of having exploited the quality of sensibility and then, still later, of exploiting its abandonment.

Ad Reinhardt had a rule (among the many rules he had, which were mainly against things) against "wiggly lines." This was probably because at the period before he made the rule he put wiggly lines in his pictures, or rather what he put in his pictures was wiggly lines. On one occasion he aired this rule in the presence of Guston who retorted that he never put wiggly lines in his pictures (more properly nothing which he ever put in his pictures was wiggly lines.)

One must distinguish that kind of painterliness (as well as that kind of response to painterliness) which is simply a matter of *delectation* over such things as loose edges, fused colors, open shapes, variations of substance, that is a purely hedonistic attitude, from those cases where possibly painterly attributes are present but serving other ends.

Pollock for example in *Lavender Mist* seems a purely delectable painter, whereas he was not always. Manet is often portrayed as delectable whereas (in contradiction to the stereotyped image of detachment) he is at almost every point *penetratingly* psychological. There are many manifestations of the *Lavender Mist* type of delectable-

Painterliness as delectation: Jackson Pollock's *Number 1, 1950 (Lavender Mist),* oil, enamel and aluminum paint on canvas, 87 inches high. Collection Alfonso Ossorio and Edward F. Dragon, East Hampton, N.Y.

Velazquez magically transforms the flat plane of the canvas in
the hair of the Infanta in *Las Meninas*, 1656 (detail). Prado, Madrid.

ness (for example in Poons); the category of delectable-ness seems in its own way a larger category than painterly since it brings together works which have painterly characteristics and those which do not. Collect all works which appeal on a purely hedonistic basis; this will include things of diverse physical characteristics. One person derives pleasure from stroking something which is smooth, another from stroking something which has curly hair; this is all pleasure from stroking.

There is a kind of standard position to the effect that one cannot speak of the meaning or import of a work of art so much as its effect upon a particular speaker. This may turn out to be the same thing. The effect may be that which I label delectation, but is by no means restricted to it. That is, delectation may carry with it other imports. That these will be neither uniformly received nor uniformly explicated is of no real matter. We should not expect our study to produce greater concreteness than the material itself warrants. It is probably the case that meaning is exactly that which means different things to different people; it is highly doubtful that it could be any other way. Not only can you not step into the same water twice, you cannot even step into it once. The union of academic and commercial requirements tends to suppress this (fact).

Pushers, pornographers and polluters talk about free-dom to be oneself. Most freedoms in use turn out to be freedom to join some group or to be autistic. There is more freedom in oil paint than anybody is able to use. That is why people turn to acrylics, collages, plastics, collaboration with engineers or businessmen.

The notion of flatness in painting, the "integrity of the picture plane," is so much academic cant, the product not of reductive art but of minimum sensibility and maximum misunderstanding. Originally it was a half-truth, an inadequate explanation or an approximation of something far more complex. In its dogmatic form as the *sine qua non* of successful modernist painting it applies only to those people who have accepted it *a priori,* dogmatically from the mouths of critics as a recipe.

One of the more ingenious rationales for flatness in painting is that it is a characteristic which only painting possesses. How beautifully this epitomizes the halfway thinking into a problem so typical of contemporary

value-scheming. In the same way as the good life is formed by an habituation to choose the good, the shallow life is formed by an habituation to choose the shallow. It is much more the case that since painting is done on a surface it possesses not only the potential, but virtually the imperative, to transform and by transforming, transform ways of feeling. Example: the hair of the Infanta in *Las Meninas. Because* it is on a flat surface we experience more deeply not only hair but all the universe in which hair exists, the space, the matter and all that. To babble about illusionism in painting as an outworn end is to fail to make necessary distinctions, and to be deliberately perverse.

The premiumization of handwriting for its own sake (again a failure to make distinctions—distinctions as to the imaginative depth of the handwriting being devoted to some end) led to a mistaken assumption that skill was a matter of dexterity only, and rather readily available. It was Analytic Cubism, through its standardization of rendering, that aimed at generalization of skill, i.e. the security, the insulation provided by a limitation of meaning and thereby produced the exaltation of will or wilfulness.

Painterly gets involved with the ambiguous and the equivocal, the variously nuanced because these are problems of the real, problems of the structure of consciousness, problems of the interplay of public and private language and their possibilities. All these are only too easy to trample underfoot for the sake of some other "efficiency." Non-painterly is always to some extent the result of an effort to suppress such factors, to feign obliviousness to them or to remain ignorant of them.

Painting wet-in-wet, which is associated with paint-erly, more importantly on the psychological than the mere manufacturing level, often has the look of just muddling. This is the same as to say that because there are no stops on a fiddle the violinist is just faking it.

While we most often associate painterly with the optical, this is not always the case. Thus late Michel-angelo is "incomplete," "open-formed," uneven, indis-tinct or distinct in unequal degree, not as "optical" translation as in the Impressionism of Rodin, but as a very precise statement of a particular state of mind. That is, there is an interchange between the sensuous and the conceptual where the concept itself takes on characteristics formerly thought to be the exclusive property of the sensuous.

It is in this way that we "resolve" the irresolutions in some kinds of late Beethoven. Or why does music at times tend to resemble speech but for the quality of gesture which it carries? Which is thus much more precisely explicative of states of consciousness. What is involved between *la la dee da DA da* and *la la dee da da DA?* Note that this is the reverse state of music from that condition to which the other arts supposedly aspire.

We ought to say several things about broken color since this is often associated with painterly.

Mr. Evans of Kodak has shown that what we would take to be the "same color" when it has a vague edge is perceived completely differently from when it has a defined edge. This is one kind of suggestion to the effect that our perception of color does not proceed passively, on a mechanistic, one-to-one basis between display and reception, but is projective and complex.

One approximation of broken-color usage, not necessarily the first in historical priority, is that it comes from a certain *goût* or delectation for an indivisible quality of experience, once found henceforth available as a useful symbol of a host of experienced properties or estimates of the world's potential. The complete iconography of Kandinsky's *Small Pleasures* would be one working out of this; several Pousette-Darts and a number of Resnicks, other ways.

One recalls vividly being smitten by the *expressiveness* of the charts for testing color-blindness in the army physical.

Broken color in Impressionism may proceed from painting leaves. It first appears in Monet's *Déjeuner sur l'Herbe*, 1865; the first glimmerings not simply of broken color as a physical technique, but also of what seems to be a corollary situation, the dawning of personalized color transformations. What do I mean by "personalized color transformations"? It means seeing into the color in a certain access of penetration such that at another moment or in another state we would not say that those colors are there. This must be sharply distinguished from other classes of color modification such as the objectively verifiable case of color modification by reflected light and the statistically verifiable case of color modification by simultaneous contrast. The phenomenon I am referring to is much more gratuitous. Sometimes it manifests itself as seeing in one and the same place, with no changes in objective conditions, two different and contradictory colors, such as violet and yellow-green, or orange and blue, even though there is no possibility that a thing can be uniformly colored and be both violet and yellow-green. Such a color transformation is in some way a *movement of the mind.* There is no doubt that this exists. It is sometimes of piercing sharpness. It is in no way the result of color blindness, but rather of color acuteness; it is very possibly closely allied to Cézanne's *"petite sensation."*

Matisse touches on something related to this when, synesthetically, he speaks of a certain blue and a certain orange being like the sound of a gong. What blue; what orange; what gong?

Now if in painting leaves the processes involved urge or permit or require both the transformation and the *goût*, what shall we say is the cause of what, not in historical but in psychological priority? (Notice for upwards of 15 years after 1865 the *ad hoc* character of Monet's paint application; that is, he does not follow a consistent technique, but employs many different methods of symbolizing sensations.) Broken color involves several kinds of equivocation about such factors.

De Kooning has spoken very eloquently (and long before his own work became truly painterly) in criticism of Courbet's "realism," showing that it was not simply where his donkey stopped that he painted, but where the qualities of wetness and dappled light had just that propensity for translation into palette-knifed paint. So is it that the compulsion for a certain kind of paint leads one to the leaves, or do the habits imposed by the process promote a habit of mind which then transvaluates a technique?

Also, in squinting at something, we do not see *those* colors more vaguely but rather other colors more distinctly.

Broken color can in some cases be a calculus of opportunities for "personal transformations." That is, since the transformation is in essence about an inner state of receipt of meaning, the occasion of each dot, each separated increment is the occasion not simply for the analysis of previously known components but for testing the *unforeseen* consequences of expression which are just coming into being. (In the same spirit Freud, when he had to make vexing decisions, flipped a coin and then examined how he felt.) Example, the Matisse divisionist *Sideboard.* Also Matisse's, the related observations that the process was too complicated to

Rodin: *Balzac*, 1895, bronze,
8 1/2 feet high. City of Antwerp.

Left: Michelangelo, *Bearded Slave*, 1527-28,
marble, 8 feet high. Accademia, Florence.

As Titian entered his late period, form begins to be dissolved in evanescent color:
Young Lady as Venus Binding the Eyes of Cupid, ca. 1550. National Gallery, Washington, D.C.

proceed on any theoretical *a priori* basis, meaning that the only testing will be teleological (i.e. in the expressiveness). Middle and late Matisse must also be seen in the light of an evolution consisting of several series of painterly transformations. The results show in paintings which are not radical in their programmatic novelty, but in what I would call their radical depth, paintings of the middle 1920s such as the *Fruits and Flowers of Nice* of which Al Held so tellingly said that Matisse uses a brush like a blunt instrument, and the Lasker *Interior with Striped Tablecloth*. Both of these display a complexity and richness of color expression brought about by a grasp of perception as a poetic process, and in so doing provide some hints as to the reading of such mysterious late works as the non-painterly *Souvenir of Oceania*.

Painterly at its most effective (and here I mean something like the *that for which* Manet sacrificed the "rationality" of the study version of his *Déjeuner sur l'Herbe* for the "irrationality" and "mistakes" of the final version) is also a reduction of redundancy, which is an interesting principle in the analysis of vision. Edwin Land has shown that for many purposes the amount of visual information which is capable of being transmitted by optical arrangements is in excess of what we require. Selectivity is a focus on particular requirements. Since the requirement is teleological (except when it is deliberately channeled by a device, as in psychological experiments), based on expression, i.e., meaning which in itself will be a projection of individual needs, what we "see" in the sense of experience is "content" as distinguished from "form," if form is shape distributions of tone and color.

The notion of the Symbolist poet Gustave Kahn that the subjective response is objectified onto the world is thus very close to the truth, but in a perhaps different

The sketch-like freedom of Velazquez' *Portrait of the Count-Duke of Olivares* (above), ca. 1638-40, 49 inches high, (Metropolitan Museum) contrasts with the formalism of the larger version, 123 inches high (left; Prado Museum, Madrid).

sense than he realized. The Symbolists (as painters the least painterly and deliberately so) and the Surrealists after them worked this out as if the objects of knowledge were perfectly clear. Proust, more sophisticated, has his painter deal with the unresolved as the actual object of experience.

So painterly probably means not to be primitive.

One of the clearest examples of redundancy reduction is that found in Rembrandt's drawings, particularly the very sparse and quick ones. In these the discontinuity of clues, gestures, space, characterization is brought together by the *a priori* continuum of the paper as the containing space in the same way that our perception of visual clues takes place in the continuum of the lived-in world. There is no question but that this reduction creates and fortifies expression. This is because it acts out the way in which we find meaning in our living experiences.

Nobody likes to deal with this type of meaning which lies outside the Panofskian tables because it is not "scientific." Precisely. It is the little flickers of non-scientific meaning which are convincing and which abide, and the scientific meanings which are ephemeral.

Painting has a greater degree of sensuous concreteness than the quick sketch (note the different status of this in Oriental art), and it articulates the symbol structure in greater complexity. (Or maybe it is the other way around; that is, in virtue of a more ramified way of symbolizing, the kinds of awareness of which we are capable is actually greater. Example, the way fleshiness is symbolized in Rembrandt and de Kooning, but not in Chinese painting.) The time difference involved in such degrees of concretization demands different means of sustaining the projective activity. Perhaps the Rembrandt sketch acts as a kind of standard for the quality of discovery. In Manet, the pell-mell activity testified to by Mallarmé may be a variant method, whereas Titian's practice of turning pictures to the wall and working on them at very widely spaced intervals accomplishes a similar end by a different route.

Performance has something to do with it. Consider what is implied in a musical performance. In any one performance the musician is permitted to pass through each indicated event but once. Every choice, every action which decides something about each event must be taken with a view to the longest structure in time and sound which will give to the separate elements the most articulate meaning.

The view of brushstroke variation as serving merely variation of tone and therefore indicative only of modeling in representation misses the point. Maybe it wishes to mistake paintings for colored reproductions of paintings. There are more intentions in modulation of brushstroke than can be indicated by modulation of tone only. The ensemble of such intentions as in the musical performance are of too great a number and too complex and too unrepeatable in their exact concatenation for a "formal" analysis. They are explained only as providing the conditions for the artist to see into the whole work.

Painterly may be more appropriate to representational painting than to abstract, not because of producing tone variations, but rather because the fact of representation itself produces a convergence of meanings, a reduction of redundancy. (With the abstract painterly, assuming there is such a thing, there is the possibility of meanings detaching themselves and flying all around so that for the sake of some resolution one entertains the field relations, the continuum itself as the only available vehicle of meaning; and this becomes submerged in what I call delectation.)

Very small changes on the objective scale can produce large differences of meaning.

Compare J. L. David's gestures with Watteau's.

Compare the two versions of the Duke of Olivares on horseback by Velazquez, one in the Metropolitan, one in the Prado. In the Met version, there is a little slatch of palette-knifed paint in the sky which creates a marvelous distance, light, palpability to the space of military and political domination. In this delivery of a specific actual, it qualifies both the physical presence and rhythm of the foreground figure and at the same time the felt meaning of the human will imposing itself upon the world of dimensions, extensions, activities and substances, and provokes a unique revery. Its poetry is that it is at the same time formal, descriptive, psychological, metaphysical. (There are other moments of this apparently off-hand transcendence of denotable ends and means; for instance the vibrant vague purple flutter in the upper right-hand corner of the *Venus and Cupid* of Titian in Washington.) This half-gram poem of paint does not occur in the Prado version; so it hangs, transfixed in time and space as a small witness to how every masterpiece is achieved by the skin of its teeth.

By Sheldon Nodelman

Roman Illusionism

Thoughts on the birth of western spatiality

Sheldon Nodelman's interests are Roman and twentieth-century painting; he teaches art history at Yale. His book on Roman Imperial portraits is to be published shortly by Yale University Press.

Roman Illusionism

Since the basic distinction between the two great cycles, antique and post-antique, which constitute Western art may be crudely summarized as that between a primarily tactile metaphoric structure and a primarily optical formation of image, it is plain that painting, which in its material two-dimensionality seems singled out as the optical art *par excellence,* must have played a major role in the development from the one into the other, and indeed all that historians of classical art have been able to infer from the evidence at their disposal confirms that this was so. Unfortunately the direct evidence—compared with what may be adduced for antique sculpture and architecture—is scanty, fragmentary and discontinuous. What Greek and Roman writers themselves describe as their major painting—the great frescoes and easel pictures of the famous masters—has totally disappeared. The structure of inferences about it which has been built up from crude reflections in provincial tombs, echoes in the graphic decoration of the minor arts, and presumed copies or at least adaptations, of debatable evidential value, in later mosaics and wall decorations, is both shaky and all too abstract.

It is doubly fortunate therefore that we have access to a large and fairly continuous sampling of painted wall decoration during a crucial phase in the development of Roman imperial art, most of it from the Campanian resort towns of Pompeii and Herculaneum and their suburbs which were preserved so miraculously for our rediscovery by the volcanic catastrophe of A.D. 79, but some of it from Rome itself, confirming that the style of the Campanian decorations was not an adventitious local phenomenon but a true reflection of that of the metropolis. While scholarly interest has long centered principally on the problems of reconstructing, from the mythological and genre pictures which are inserted into the framework of these wall-decorative schemes, the appearance of putative Greek originals, it has become increasingly evident that most of these pictures are products of the age in which they were in fact executed, at most freely adapting and transforming motifs from earlier masterpieces, and are carefully integrated spatially and coloristically into the the decorative ensembles to which they pertain. Few of the Campanian *quadri* rose above artisan quality, but the pictured architectural

schemes of wall decoration of which they form a part are themselves not only often imposing and sophisticated but, properly examined, may be of immense aid to a proper understanding of the over-all development of Roman art during the century and a half from which most of them stem. This period, from the second half of the first century B.C. to the late first century A.D., saw the synthesis from its native and Hellenistic roots of a truly Roman art, henceforth metropolitan with respect to the older Mediterranean centers, an art which was to serve as the vital matrix out of which our later Western art would develop. Quite aside from the intrinsic beauty and fascination of the painted wall programs, and the glimpse they afford us of the ideological horizons, the poetic and emotional ideals of those who commissioned them—contemporaries of Cicero, Catullus, Virgil, Horace and Seneca—they afford us a sharpened insight into the central problems of contemporary form, problems which appear perhaps less explicitly, more ambiguously in the increasingly pictorialized plastic structure of the major coeval monuments of architecture and sculpture.

At the end of the nineteenth century the great German scholar August Mau systematized the large corpus of Campanian wall decorations into four phases, each distinguished by a different syntax of fictive architectural and ornamental elements and by a different relationship between the illusionary system and the actual plane of the wall. Despite the anomalies inherent in the application of so simple a scheme to a large, various and continuously evolving body of wall-painting, and despite continuing scholarly dispute as to the exact chronological boundaries of the four styles and even as to the contemporaneity or chronological succession of the third and fourth (only recently finally resolved in favor of the latter alternative), these distinctions have remained in use. Mau's Style I, which prevails in the Campanian houses of the third and second centuries, down to about 80 B.C. is not properly speaking illusionistic in character, or only so to the most limited degree. It consists of the careful imitation in paint and stucco of the rare materials and powerful, drafted ashlar masonry, adorned with decorated cornices and pilasters, which made resplendent the hewn and squared walls of shrines, palaces and great public buildings. This is not inherently a Roman system; it had long been current in the Hellenistic East, whence indeed derived the architectural forms which it reproduced. There is however one significant difference between Style I wall systems in East and West: in the Greek world the architectural logic of the masonry wall is carefully repeated in the painted and stuccoed imitation, while in Italy the great upright slabs, the *orthostats,* which properly form the base of the wall, were soon themselves elevated on a socle to constitute its center, their polished surfaces and rare materials being attributed a quasi-pictorial value. The luminous zone thus constituted would later be articulated into an illusionary space inhabited by fictive architectures and figures.

The second Pompeiian style and those which follow and are developed from it are of wholly different order, concerned with the expansion of the wall plane into a realm of architectural and sacral-mythological fantasy, thus transforming the space in which the observer stands from the context of daily life onto an exalted, even divinized plane. The earliest, and most rudimentary, wall program in Style II so far known comes not from one of the Campanian centers but from Rome, in the so-called *House of the Griffins,* an aristocratic residence of the first years of the first century B.C. on the Palatine Hill, preserved for us when it was buried in the massive terracing operations necessary for the erection of the great palace of the Emperor Domitian whose ruins dominate the Palatine to this day. Style II and its successors are native Roman inventions, whose influence appears only later, and sporadically, in the Hellenistic

Earliest known example of Style II: Wall in the House of the Griffins, an aristocratic residence on the Palatine Hill, Rome, 80-60 B.C.

Detail of historical frieze with life-size figures, dining-room, Publius Sinistor Villa, Boscoreale, ca. 40 B.C. Naples Museum.

lands. It is the pictorial equivalent to that other great Roman plastic invention, the relief in graduated planes, whose definitive formulation was delayed—unless this be attributed merely to the accidents of preservation—until the end of the century, in the *Ara Pacis* of Augustus.

One of the most impressive programs of Style II decoration to have survived—in regrettably fragmentary form and dispersed among several collections—once decorated a country villa at Boscoreale, known to have belonged to one Publius Fannius Sinistor and dating from about 40 B.C. A dining-room of this house was ennobled with a great frieze of life-size painted figures—the exact iconography is still a matter of dispute—which like its even more famous contemporaries, the Dionysiac frieze of the Villa of Mysteries at Pompeii and the great Odyssey landscape frieze now in the Vatican Library, is a copy from an earlier, Hellenistic cycle, and like the former was set against a resplendent backdrop of "Pompeiian" red. But the frieze's original relation to the viewer and to the wall upon which it lay is utterly altered. It is inserted into a painted architecture whose relation to the actual wall is complex and ambiguous. Upon a low socle (not visible in the photograph) whose spatial position is identical with the actual plane of the wall, great columns whose drums bear ornamented

Drawing of Boscoreale wall decoration showing trompe-l'oeil columns with bosses, dramatizing the painted architecture.

29

Back and right walls of the cubiculum of the Boscoreale Villa, ca. 40 B.C.,
with stage-set townscapes and perspectives of sacred buildings. Metropolitan Museum.

bosses rise the full height of the wall and lock themselves firmly into what the spectator may take to be his own space—projecting forward into it, indeed, since the flat socle well below eye level, with its indication of literal spatial position, is easily forgotten in the face of the dramatic emphasis and compositional prominence given to the columns. If the columns, which strive to appear as though they are in fact supporting the ceiling of the room, seem to project forward toward the spectator, the plane of the horizontal frieze behind them is readily identified with the real bounding plane of the spectator's space. This identification is reinforced by the two dominant horizontals, the painted moulding and the Doric frieze and cornice which bound this zone below and above, and which expand laterally across the full width of the wall as horizontal counterparts to the columns. A closer look however reveals that the framing horizontals themselves cannot be in the same plane: the solid, richly modeled figures are deployed in a shallow stage space, indicated by a dark strip at the bottom of

the frieze, and therefore the red wall behind them, and the frieze and cornice which crown it, are firmly set back behind the plane of the lower molding. Behind the screen wall against which the figures are deployed is visible yet another cornice and architrave, borne on their own perspectively diminished colonnade—Doric now instead of Corinthian—and alternately running parallel to the fictive wall in front, or deepening into perspectives of columnar halls back into space.

Thus the spectator is allowed a glimpse—though no more than a glimpse, through a narrow aperture set high up on the wall and, even within the terms of the illusion, only visually but not physically attainable—of a deep space *behind* what he has been led provisionally to identify as the true boundary plane of the room. That boundary plane is now visible as merely a screening wall, while fugitive vistas beyond tempt the imagination into delicious spatial fantasies of indefinite extent, whose transcendent nature is hinted at by the sacral associations of the architectural forms. The atmosphere of yearning and nostalgic reverie which is here created—so familiar in the poetry of later antiquity—depends of course on the withholding of any more than an intimation of these ideal distances, and so the view into the perspectival depths of columnar halls which open out behind the screen wall is interrupted by what appear to be little architecturally framed figural scenes; painted reproductions in fact of votive pictures of the kind dedicated in sanctuaries, their covering wings thrown open, which firmly reassert the screen wall's plane. Moreover, as doubly illusory—paintings of paintings—and as vehicles of a new ambiguity of scale and distance, they will assume an increasingly important role in the subsequent development of the illusory wall systems.

Much the same basic system is evident in the splendidly preserved *cubiculum* or bed chamber of the Boscoreale villa, now installed in the Metropolitan Museum, with its stage-set townscapes and perspectives of sacral architecture. Here too the wall surface is rhythmically scanned by great chiaroscurally painted pilasters which feign to be part of the literal architecture of the wall, running from the floor to the entablature which supports the vaulted ceiling, corner to corner, firmly anchoring the illusory system into the actual space. Here too a high socle blocks the possibility of entry into the fictive depths, and in general, each successive plane of depth opens out at correspondingly greater height, less and less available to direct access, more and more attainable by the eye alone. In this a notable role is played by the catenary curves of the dark hangings visible above the screen walls blocking access into the columnar portico, with its little circular temple: their unusual scalloped curvature stridently asserts the wall's flatness against the beckoning depths beyond, and

Detail of the famous Odyssey frieze, *Ulysses in the Land of the Lestrygonians,* from a house on the Esquiline Hill, Rome, ca. 40 B.C. (about 55 inches high). Vatican Library, Rome.

Augustus and His Retinue, detail of the *Ara Pacis,* Rome, 13-9 B.C. The foreground
figures stand out against an illusionistic system of graduated planes.

indeed the curves sharpen markedly to counteract the
corresponding recessive flight of the colonnades.

By the use of large "architectural" elements which
are scaled and ordered closely to correspond with the
actual space, and to which the viewer can relate
physically in a very direct way, as the jumping-off point
for a play of vibrating planes of depth, the mature
Second Style usurps the physical reality of the wall and
subverts it into illusory depth. It relates to the actual
wall, that is, in its character as real object, of material
plane, as all previous antique art had done, and not to a
framed-off ideal plane of representation whose au-
tonomy is gained, as in the art of our own post-antique
tradition, by the sacrifice of that direct physical
connection with the spectator. This fundamental
distinction, which Riegl noted long ago, accounts for
the absolute structural disparity between classical and,
e.g., Renaissance painting: in the former the perspectival
organization of the figures, both internally and with
respect to one another, their positioning with respect to
the bounding plane and its rectilinear limits, and the
distribution of light and shadow, all more or less
directly follow from the relation of the individual figure
to the material plane, of which it is in some sense an
emanation, a particularization of the energies resident
within it, and never in principle a denial of it. In
painting of the later Western tradition—the definitive
formulation is Giotto's—the figurative system is ideally,
self-referentially organized; it exists upon, but is not of,
the nature of, the subjacent physical plane.

This accounts for the easy, tensionless spreading out
of forms across the available space so striking in antique
figural painting, and so unlike the taut, rhythmic
relationship, with which we are more familiar, between an
assertedly autonomous representational system and the
sharply defined limits at which it ceases to obtain. It
accounts also for the much-disputed and lamented
"failure" of Greek and Roman artists to employ a
"legitimate construction" in perspective. Quite aside
from theoretical questions of geometry, the fundamental assumptions of their representational system
were totally incompatible with an infinite spatial mani-
fold conceived as logically prior to the objects disposed
within it, and draining those objects of their direct,
ineluctable physical presence. This authority of immediate tangible presence was enjoyed by the represented
object in its quality as an expression or emanation of
the physical forces active in the material object which
was the ground of the representation, and its legitimacy
was expressed through the object's "own" vanishing
point, or points, which directly related it to that
ground. An extensive space could be represented only
mediately, in the ambiguous and shifting relationships
between the various space cells, each with its local
perspective "system," generated by the juxtaposition
of represented objects. Such a space can be readily seen

in the Boscoreale townscapes, in the landscapes and townscapes of the reliefs of the column of Trajan, and (etherealized by atmospheric perspective) in the paintings of the Odyssey cycle in the Vatican.

It is of the nature of such a system that it renounces total logical consistency; the eye is constantly reminded of the life-giving relationship between the represented object and the material plane, in a fashion which recalls to us that of Cubist painting. The ambiguities of position are not so much between a plane of representation and planes diagonally recessive from it, as in analytic Cubism, as between the material plane and illusory parallel planes forward and back of it. Cubist painting indeed represents a key stage in the dismantling of that illusionary system toward which the spatial experiments of the Boscoreale paintings and their successors, still employing the conventions of classical formal structure even as they strive to transcend them, were to lead. Here the identification of the plane of representation with the material plane still visible in Cubist painting—or rather the domination and virtual absorption of the latter by the former—has not yet occurred; the integrity of the material plane must be preserved so that the illusory planes generated from it may be infused with its authority. Thus the painted architecture of the Boscoreale rooms seeks to ground itself firmly in the actual space and upon the material walls of these rooms, and to modulate the inevitable contradictions—especially visible at corners and intersections of planes—between the actual and illusory spatial systems, by successively polyvalent readings, so that at each transition of illusory plane, access to the material plane may seem but a step away. Thus a rich sensation of spatial openness and multi-positionality is created which throbs with a physicality directly derived from the motor-kinesthetic sensibility of the beholder.

In its basic dispositions this spatial system closely corresponds to the momentous formulation in Augustan times of the illusionist relief system of graduated planes as we see it in the processional panels of the *Ara Pacis (Altar of Peace)* in Rome (B.C. 13-9). Here for the first time in antiquity one does not first perceive the relief ground as the object *per se* in terms of which the observer spatially locates himself, and from which, as isolated projections, the figures derive their plastic substance. Instead it is the forwardmost plane of serried, togate figures who—like the big, forward columns of Boscoreale—assert the most decisive plastic authority, and like them are alone firmly anchored above and below to the physical frame of the illusionary system. Each of the successive, clearly discriminated planes which are staggered back in depth behind the first—like the painted series of parallel planes receding from the wall—is shallower in plasticity until the ground plane, like the final, glimpsed depths at Boscoreale, is dissolved into atmosphere, into a free space of indefinite extent. And again like Boscoreale each shift back into illusory depth is accompanied by progressively more restricted

Late Style II: House of Livia, Palatine, Rome, ca. 30 B.C., with decoration centered around an illusionist votive picture.

Reconstruction of wall painting in the Homeric House, Pompeii. The blank space in the center contained a mythological scene.

access for the eye (and, metaphorically, for the physical entrance of the spectator) until the uttermost depth is merely glimpsed hauntingly through the interstices of the foreground system. Though its full implications for plastic structure were not to be rigorously implemented for two centuries more, this system with its drastic

Transitional Style III-IV: Corner of the banquet room of the House of the Vettii, Pompeii, ca. A.D. 62-68.

displacement of plastic emphasis from the core to the periphery of the sculptured object marks a fateful shift toward a new, space-dominated conception of representational structure.

Despite the fundamental similarities referred to above, it is easy to see that the reliefs of the *Ara Pacis* by no means compare *stylistically* to the Boscoreale frescoes of a generation before. For a more intimate correlation we have only to look at the wall-decorative systems which were in fact roughly contemporary with it, those of the late Second Style and its transition to the Third. We are fortunate to be able to follow this evolution at its source in some detail from a series of magnificent wall paintings executed in Rome, under the highest court patronage, as well as from Campanian examples. A splendid wall from the so-called House of Livia on the Palatine, probably part of the official residence of Augustus himself, represents this phase as does one from the Homeric House at Pompeii. The system of Style II as we were familiar with it at Boscoreale has notably evolved. Most evident is the reorganization of the wall around a strongly centered pavilion or *aedicula,* which contains a framed mythological picture (that in the Homeric House has been destroyed). Such pictures-within-pictures, which share the elongated proportions characteristic of the wall system on a whole, add the piquancy of double illusion to the scheme, especially as they are often so designed and framed as to leave room for doubt whether they are not windows through the wall into a deep space behind, like the similarly shaped slot views of architecture and landscape which pierce the wall to either side of them; thus the whole status of the illusion is put in question. While the large-scale architectural members of the earlier Second Style had been regularly distributed to lock into the real space of the room and had therefore to stress the architecturally crucial corners, the new pavilion system concentrates plastic emphasis in the center of the wall and draws the spectator's attention away from the sides. As a result there is a tendency for the illusionary wall system to detach itself from the actual walls upon which it is emplaced and to constitute itself as a seamless envelope of illusion, coextensive with, but in no way implicated in the materiality of the material walls which it overlays. This process of detachment can be seen in more advanced form in the virtual negation of the corners in a room of the Pompeiian House of the Vettii which stands at the interface of the Third and

Style III, illusionist architecture reduced to ornament: Villa
of Agrippa Postumus, Boscotrecase, after 11 B.C. Naples Museum.

Fourth Styles; its ultimate consequence is the insubstantial, shimmering web of mosaic which utterly
dematerializes the interior architecture of the great
Early Christian churches.

This dematerializing tendency is evident also in the
attenuation and elongation of the fictive architectural
members and by their dissolution at crucial junctures
into precious ornamental configurations. The big,
solid members and ostensibly clear, if finally contradictory, spatial divisions of earlier Style II are replaced
by a multiplication of smaller elements and an insistence
on the recession of orthogonals into depth while the
planes parallel to the material wall surface are likewise
multiplied and broken up, so that the impression of a
continuous lateral expanse derivative of, and thus
reasserting in sublimated form, the real wall plane, is
diminished. The device of the little framed votive
picture, whose tell-tale presence was noted already at
Boscoreale, is repeated, and reinforced now by a
multitude of figural motifs, masks, caryatids, statues,
sometimes legitimized as architectural ornament but

sometimes seemingly inhabiting the interior of the
pavilion system as real creatures. At many positions and
of inconsistently varying sizes, these animated figures
not only generate cells of enlivened space around
themselves but help subvert any coherent sense of scale,
thus further dematerializing the painted architectural
system and denying it any stable spatial relation to the
observer.

The reduction of scale, multiplication of parts,
ornamentalizing tendencies and the fluttering of the
superimposed planes within narrow limits characteristic
of the late Second Style are noticeable in the processional reliefs of the *Ara Pacis* as also in the portraiture
of this period, notably that of Augustus himself. These
"excesses" so far removed from the structural sobriety
of real architecture, incurred the wrath of Vitruvius, the
tough old military engineer who was writing his famous
architectural treatise during the heyday of the late
Second Style. Indeed the severity and order which
distinguish the Third Style in its earlier phase—it is
documentable before 12 B.C.—are commonly regarded

as the signs of a classicistic reaction to such "excess" in keeping with the conservative tone of so many aspects of Augustan culture. From the standpoint of conscious ideological intent this is no doubt so, but viewed within the context of the structural development of ancient art, the innovations of the Third Style appear not so much a denial of the illusionist aspirations of the Second as a radical fulfillment of them. The plane of the wall, it is true, is reasserted in all its flatness. The elaborate apparatus of fictive architecture and glimpsed vistas has dwindled to an exiguous framework of delicate, ornamental pilasters and cornices, much too thin and flat to be thought of as involved in any real architectural task or to be physically empathized with by the beholder, which still form a spindly *aedicula* round a dematerialized landscape or classicistic mythological scene. An air of elegant preciosity and cool "correctness" replaces the exuberance of the Second Style. But the wall plane which is so severely "reasserted" here is neither the painted wall of the First Style with its careful mimesis of a massive ashlar construction, nor the real wall with the architectonic forces inherent in it. Instead it is a weightless plane dissected by its taut, linear articulation into a pattern of flat, rectangular panels whose refulgent, saturated colors and reflective surfaces deny them any materiality in favor of an

Wall painting of the Augustan Age: "Black Room" of the Farnesina Villa, Rome, ca. 19 B.C. National Museum, Rome.

Style IV, ultimate dematerialization of the wall in the Age of
Nero: Ixion Room, House of the Vettii, A.D. 70-79. Pompeii.

indeterminate, chromatic spatiality. That these severely delimited panels are in fact infused with a kind of atmospheric space is made clear by their role as an ambient medium not only for delicate ornamental candelabra and garlands but for little flying creatures, nymphs and genii, or even for insubstantial, transparent landscapes, as in the Farnesina Villa "Black Room."

This new mode of spatiality is achieved without any of the illusionist devices of the Second Style, devices which depended at last resort upon the spectator's initial perception of the solid physical presence of the material wall and which echoed it repeatedly. These intimations of physicality are now dissolved in an insubstantial chromatic glow. The reasserted wall plane is no longer even derivatively the physical plane; the surface becomes an independent optical entity without reference to that internal core of mass of which, formerly, it was the expression. In a process momentous for the later history of Western art, the plane of representation is beginning to infuse and transform the material plane itself.

The later evolution of Roman wall painting systems, so far as it can be followed, pursues and extends this epochal innovation. (In properly transposed terms, the same evolution is visible as well in reliefs and in sculptures in the round.) The Fourth Style, created during the reign of Nero and still current in later form when Vesuvius' eruption in 79 put an end to our Campanian evidence, is conventionally regarded as a return to the boisterous extravagances of the Second Style after the chilly rigors of the Third. An examination of a Fourth Style wall system such as that in the gorgeous Room of Ixion in the House of the Vettii makes clear the superficiality of such a view. Active and rich in contrasts as it is, and employing once again such Second Style apparatus as slots opening into deep perspective views and ornate columns and entablatures on or seemingly in front of the plane of the wall, the absolute dominance of that plane in optical terms, firmly established by the Third Style, is never called into question. Nor is the old, material plane localizable any more as the generative core of the illusive planes. The architectural members are as thin and fugitive as the most attenuated ones of the expiring Second Style, and with much less ambition toward spatial recession. Shallow pavilions quiver ambiguously in front of bright surface panels. The narrow slots of deep perspective

views are isolated cut-outs, in no way compromising the over-all continuity of the plane. In fact they enhance its insubstantiality, declaring it not the outer surface of a solid mass (as one might still perhaps, if somewhat perversely, try to read it in early Style III) but a mere screen, paper-thin, punched with holes, with empty space behind. Thus the surface is cut off from any claim to the plastic authority of actual mass, and the spatial vistas themselves are too limited and isolated to excite the tactile sensations which might be evoked by the expectation of physical accessibility. They are carefully placed too high on the wall for that. The vertical and horizontal continuities of the articulating members, by which the Second Style linked its illusory space with the actual, and which persisted in the strict if pencil-thin linear divisions of the Third, are here nowhere to be found above the level of the low socle. Deprived of such integration and isolated by heavy frames the individual panels, whether simulating marble inlay "on" the wall, shallow pavilions in front of it, spatial glimpses or pictures-within-pictures of varying sizes and spatial implications, are perceived separately, vibrating spatially back and forth in relation to their neighbors in an effect of effulgent and incalculable richness. They are in fact visually bound together much less strongly to one another (lest the continuity thus created retain for the spectator any implication of a fixed material plane of definite spatial distance from him) than each separately is to the beholder. He is confronted thus by an immaterial world of visions which cannot be localized in physical space. He is moreover the center of that world, whose delicious if baffling inconstancies seem to depend upon his momentary subjective reactions rather than any set of stable, ascertainable external relations.

The spatial possibilities inherent in these Fourth Style innovations were to be extended and refined in later antiquity into even greater immateriality, ending in a total reorganization of the elements of representation. Though centuries were yet to elapse before this evolution was complete, the significance of what has been recounted here for the subsequent emergence of the spatial ideal of modern Western art will not escape the reader. Only after the stubborn presence of the material plane had been thoroughly sublimated into an indeterminate optical expanse could a new mode of representation be called into being, a self-contained system of ideal relations based upon the idea of infinite space.

By Terisio Pignatti

The Great Venetians

"Painterly" light and color occur as natural phenomena in Venice

Prof. Terisio Pignatti is the Director of the Museo Correr,
Venice; he recently published a major book on Giorgione.

The Great Venetians

"The mosaics on the walls, the *opus tessellatum* on the floors, have something of the sea about them in their washed brightness: as though the tide had just gone down from those churches built on the seashore or on islands, leaving behind it layers of stranded shingle, speckled pebbles, chips of iridescent shell, their design still bearing the mark of the curved path of the waves..."

This is Venice in the words of one of her recent scholars, Sergio Bettini: a magic world, in which the element of color is a sort of underlay above which poetic forms emerge as if it were a process of nature. No doubt nature plays a part in the Venetian intellectual landscape, made up as it is of elements so full of color, so various and so evocative. And in a sense, the environment itself could be taken as a typical example of what we mean by the "picturesque": it is like a sudden, constantly surprising *improvviso* under the effect of changing lights and seasons.

Is it possible that the watery, mirror-like phenomenon of the city and its lagoons has transmitted its characteristics to the style of her artists? Venetian art, notably its architecture and painting, has in fact often been described as essentially "anti-geometric," and scholars have agreed with this. The painters even caused perspective to fade out, so that images "multiplied, entwined, broke down and built up, and finally left the spectator with nothing but fields of blue and gold, marked only on the shifting, exultant notation of an endless song of color."

Thus it is possible that the *picturesque* element in the Venetian environment was transmuted into the *painterly* element in Venetian art. Leaving aside the problem of architecture, we would like to follow up this principle in a few major examples of the activity of great painters, in order to establish how they operated within the context of this situation, and to see whether we can draw a conclusion as to there being a similarity of language among them due to their way of understanding "creative color" or what we should like to call "painterly color."

From where, and how far back can we trace the origins of painterly painting in Venice? I would say from its very beginnings, from the ancient mosaics of

San Marco. Dating mostly from the mid-thirteenth century, they coincide often with the basic interpretation of the Venetian figurative vocabulary, which relies on the element of a creative color. We may mention the delicate, softly hazed atmosphere of the *Prayer in the Orchard,* or even more the mosaics of the narthex, showing episodes of the Flood. What is more persuasively painterly than the touched, spotty, refracted rainbow which peeps through the stripes of the rainfall, announcing the end of the storm? Where else in the Romanesque world do we find such multi-colored birds as the ones which flutter out of the Ark, with Noah smiling over them like a satisfied trainer? We cannot escape the sensation that the white of the dove bringing good news to Noah, or the fresh sinuous movement of the sea-waves, was obtained with a direct, sensitive imagination that relied basically on the immediate effect of the radiant pigments of the mosaic itself. Creative color, therefore, is at the very beginnings of Venetian art.

The masters who better than any others interpret the message of San Marco mosaics are perhaps Gentile Bellini and Carpaccio. The latter particularly condenses his vision in a soft, painterly touch. It may seem obvious to quote such miracles of color as the St. Ursula canvases at the Accademia: the *Dream of the Saint* in her room, where a cool morning light glazes in perfect silence the walls and the sophisticated furniture, or softly bathes the paneling and tapestries. The fascinating little sketch for the large canvas, now at the Uffizi, proves how intelligently Carpaccio used light and its creative effects: a crisp triangle of brightness through an open door, a dense shadow which tones down the area in the corner, the striking spotted shape of the pet dog, sharp and spirited.

That Carpaccio predicted a sort of sketchy, Rococo-like touch, becomes evident in many backgrounds of his paintings. We can point to the polychromatic field of furred and feathered caps of the waiting gentlemen in *The Return of the Ambassadors,* or the swaying figure of the gondolier gently propelling his boat over the lagoon framed through the arcades of the *Arrival of the Ambassadors.* Both examples reveal the artist's use of fluid brush strokes, here and there heightened with pure white, or thicker dots of red or blue pigment. The immediate result is a peculiar painterly liveliness which goes much further than one might have thought possible for a pupil of the Bellinis, who basically depend on their

The most faithful portrait of his times: Detail of Canaletto's *The Doge and Officials Visiting the Scuola San Rocco*, to celebrate the deliverance of Venice from the plague of 1575-76.

Detail of *The Flood*, 13th-century mosaic
in the narthex of San Marco, Venice.

Carpaccio's sketch for *The Dream of St.
Ursula*, ca. 1490-95. Uffizi, Florence.

Carpaccio: *The Reception of the English Ambassadors*, detail
from the Legend of St. Ursula, 1496-98. Accademia, Venice.

Veronese's palette assumes a quality of sparkle and glitter that rivals all his contemporaries: Detail from the *Baptism and Temptation of Christ*. The Brera, Milan.

characteristic use of chiaroscuro hatching, overpainted with colored pigments, but keyed to the tactile values of a plastic image in the Tuscan tradition.

Were Carpaccio's contemporaries aware of the message of this unique style of coloring, which was inaugurating the basis of the modern Venetian School? A positive reply may only be found in the masters of the last generation of the Quattrocento, such as Giorgione (born ca. 1477) and Titian (born ca. 1490). Giorgione was certainly impressed by the sketchy manner in Carpaccio's little background figures as can be seen in the *Allendale Adoration* in Washington, or the Uffizi panels. Moreover I believe that we can find a connecting link with the "painterly" in such drawings (or imaginary drawings) by Giorgione as the ones we can detect in his *Castelfranco Frieze:* a saint, a shepherd, a nude female, which all show the hatched, striped touch of Carpaccio's pen-and-brush technique.

We can clearly agree that Giorgione falls easily within the definition of painterly painting, especially in his late works (ca. 1508-10). Although there always remains in his style a fund of Bellinesque chiaroscuro, there are periods in his work which are almost purely painterly. Leaving aside the obvious example of the *Tempestà,* we can notice this quality in the *Philosophers,* especially the face of the oldest man (Aristotle?), whose painterly shadows add a mysterious touch of distant loneliness to that noble figure (Edgar Wind now explains this as an allusion to the celestial habitation of the soul). A close study of the very few remaining drawings by Giorgione also makes it clear that the painterly elements of the Vienna panel are consciously derived from the master's style. One can prove it by comparing the loose treatment of the Philosopher's head with the shaded impasto of such sheets as the newly attributed *Philosopher* of Christ Church (Oxford), or the moving *Old Man's Head* from a Swiss private collection. In such works the outlines are practically lost, the hatching is reduced to a brush-like graded shading, so that the result comes very close to the one in the painting.

Thus it is evident that Giorgione approaches the painterly through a soft, diffused tonalism, through a skillful blend of pigment and light, with chalk, pencil or brush aiming at a *sfumato* effect which quickly becomes

Giorgione: *Old Man's Head,* black chalk on paper. Private collection, Zurich.

Giorgione: *The Three Philosophers,* detail, ca. 1508. Kunsthistorisches Museum, Vienna.

Light to achieve an effect of realistic immediacy: Detail of Titian's *Man with a Glove,* ca. 1520. Louvre

The geometry of the buildings becomes dissolved in atmospheric color: Francesco Guardi's *The Grand Canal at the Pescheria, Venice,* 29 1/2 inches high. Brera, Milan.

The proud *improvviso* of Titian's brush:
The Annunciation, detail. S. Salvador, Venice.

Titian: *Man on Horseback and Fallen Warrior*,
charcoal. Graphische Sammlung, Munich.

G. B. Tiepolo: *Virgin and Child with St. Joseph*,
pen and brown wash. Collection R. Heinemann, New York.

his special characteristic. Vasari, when writing of Giorgione and Titian in 1568, describes this central development of Giorgione as the one which most impressed the young Titian.

Titian clearly continued the art of his master after Giorgione's sudden death in 1510, but with a different approach. A born realist, he probably secretly admired the frightening imagination and sometimes brutal naturalism which Dürer demonstrated in Venice during his stay in 1505-7. Therefore, Titian's painterly painting adds to Giorgione's control of subdued light a flashing, bolder, dramatic touch. Compare the landscape of the *Tempestà* with one of Titian's earliest backgrounds, for example the view of a city among the hills in his *Orpheus and Eurydice* (from Bergamo). Here we witness a ripening of the painterly effect, even a sort of picturesque, which will not flourish until two centuries later in the romantic *Ruins* of a Marco Ricci.

Indeed, the tendency to paint without outlines becomes more and more peculiar to Titian's style in the first decades of the Cinquecento. Even when he designs monumental compositions, like the *Miracles of St. Anthony* in Padua (1511), he allows his brush to wander freely along the picture surface, building the massive figures of his characters in a proud *improvviso*, while pigments are applied to the surface with dash and fluency. Where else in the early Cinquecento would we find such a hand as in the *Man with the Glove* (Louvre), which perhaps only Velazquez, more than a century later, was able to assimilate? In Titian's painterly style, for the first time light is used to achieve an effect of realistic immediacy, of spontaneity, with an extraordinarily free touch, not to mention an intensity of tone freed from any surviving restraint of the chiaroscuro drawing—at a time when the latter still was the rule in Florence and Rome.

As for Titian's drawings, there are no better confirmations of his painterly style. They look like paintings; in fact they *are* paintings, where the charcoal stroke is substituted for the dark pigments, while heightening with the white chalk enriches them with the liveliest effects of atmospheric reality.

The crisis of Mannerism, which affected Titian in the last phase of his life (after the 1550s), added a further

G. B. Tiepolo: *Africa* (detail), fresco ceiling of the staircase, Würzburg Residenz, 1752-53.

G. B. Tiepolo: Detail from the *Crowning with Thorns*, ca. 1738-40. Church of S. Alvise, Venice.

development to the painterly characteristics of his work. Space itself becomes a shaky, unstable representation; highlights become increasingly dramatic, tied to a whirlpool of directions. Fragmented and dotted, summary and loose, the technique of the late Titian can be matched only by the anguished touch of the old Rembrandt.

Parallel with Titian's painterly development is the artistic process of his younger contemporaries: Bassano, Tintoretto and Veronese. The painterly principle is most evident with Jacopo Bassano, in such sketches as the *Head of an Apostle* (Albertina) or the changing, rich textures of pigments in such middle-period paintings as the San Teonisto *Crucifixion* (Treviso), or the dazzling *St. Roch* (Brera). By contrast, it may be more difficult to assess the painterly qualities in Tintoretto, where they blend with a basic respect for Mannerist plasticism, and an intense feeling for religious subjects. Still, when the artist allowed himself a moment of freedom, he produced startling masterpieces in a completely painterly manner, as in the detail of the little background figure of the spinner in the *Last Supper,* in the Scuola di San Rocco, where the fluid pigments flame white-hot.

Strangely enough, more than to his direct followers like his son Domenico or his pupil Palma Giovane,

Tintoretto's painterly heritage descends to an artist of the 1650s, Francesco Maffei. Some of his most Baroque works, like the dazzling *Assumption* now in the Vicenza Museum, seem to condense the highest effects of the painterly manner, in an extreme freedom of handling. Although an eclectic, Maffei's personality is essentially a sort of distillation of the Baroque, without a complete abandonment of the traditional techniques of the sixteenth-century Venetian school. The classic example of the latter is Paolo Veronese, perhaps the master in which the Venetian painterly qualities reach the most modern and striking interpretation.

Veronese's education was in fact based upon the finest expression of Mannerism in Northern Italy: Giulio Romano's frescoes, Raphael's tapestries in Mantua, Correggio's work in Parma and Sammicheli's architecture in Verona. His capacity to construct a human form or an architectonic background therefore goes much further than the Venetian school, and integrates formal elements that show him as a very independent artist in the city of the lagoons, where he settled shortly after 1550. However, Paolo Veronese also had a particular interest in Venetian colorism which he probably admired in Titian, leading him to a very personal interpretation of the painterly principle and,

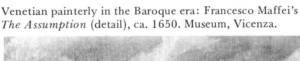

Venetian painterly in the Baroque era: Francesco Maffei's *The Assumption* (detail), ca. 1650. Museum, Vicenza.

Jacopo Bassano: *Head of an Apostle,* charcoal, red crayon and pastel. Albertina, Vienna.

Left: G. B. Tiepolo, *The Triumph of Venus,* sketch for a lost ceiling. Prado, Madrid.

Flame-like fluid pigments: detail of Tintoretto's
The Last Supper, ca. 1562-66. S. Trovaso, Venice.

Pietro Longhi: *The Morning Cup of Chocolate* (detail),
ca. 1774-80. Cà Rezzonico, Venice.

The Venetian Rococo spread to all Europe from works like
G. A. Pellegrini's *Venus and Cupid.* Private Collection, Venice.

Pietro Longhi: *Lady and Gentleman on a Divan*, black and
white chalk on buff paper. Correr Museum, Venice.

G. A. Pellegrini: *Europe*, pen and
wash. National Museum, Stockholm.

Canaletto: *The Old Fish Market*, Venice,
pen drawing. Philadelphia Museum.

Francesco Guardi: *The Grand Canal Looking toward S. Stae*,
pen and wash drawing. Coll. Richard S. Davis, London.

Francesco Guardi's *Piazza San Marco during
the Sensa Fair*, ca. 1776. Kunsthistorisches Museum, Vienna.

perhaps, developing it to the utmost of its possibilities. Endowed with a brilliant, sophisticated mind and inclined toward an exalted sense of beauty, Veronese's palette from his earliest works assumes a quality of sparkle and glitter of pigments that rivals all his contemporaries. Even working in terms of the most carefully developed forms, he is able to remodel them with his radiant palette, and transmute them with his colors. Their key is unmistakable: cold and silvery, mellow but always bright, woven with light, supremely exciting yet touched with total unreality, a sort of abstraction. Any detail from his frescoes or canvases in San Sebastiano in Venice will demonstrate that: from the soft reflections in the altarpiece of *Saints Adoring the Virgin,* to the crystalline episodes of the armed soldiers in the *Martyrdom of St. Sebastian.*

If we attempt to trace the influence of Veronese's painterly style in the following centuries, G.B. Tiepolo must be recalled first. The most famous decorator of eighteenth-century Venice, when examined in the framework of the painterly principle, appears in direct filiation to the great painter of the Palladian villas and the new Palazzo Ducale, Paolo Veronese. From Veronese, Tiepolo borrowed the fluent oil pigments supported but not overwhelmed by majestic compositions and a high theatrical mood. The sparkle we find in his *Africa* frescoes at Würzburg has a distant origin in the San Sebastiano figures of Veronese, but renewed by Tiepolo's technique and style. To reconfirm, it is enough to look at one of the most fascinating Tiepolo drawings, in the style of the *Madonna and Child* of the R. Heinemann collection, New York. The artist's understanding of painterly color is evident in the bright contrast of clear and shaded areas, where the clear ones reveal themselves as blank paper, and the shadows assume all the tonal vibrations of glazed silvery or golden colors.

Tiepolo concludes a period in Venetian painting of the Settecento, where the painterly manner is the unique means of expression, the main reason why the Venetian school is famous in all Europe, contending only with France for primacy. Since the beginning of

Climax of the painterly in the Age of Elegance: Details from Gian Antonio Guardi's *Aurora,* an over-door panel decoration, ca. 1755-60. Collection Vittorio Cini, Venice.

the eighteenth century, indeed, such masters as Sebastiano Ricci and Pellegrini brought the Venetian manner to England, the Low Countries, Germany and Paris. What can be more painterly than such a dappled sketch by Pellegrini as *Europa* (Stockholm), or more persuasively attractive than one of his blonde beauties, so filled with Arcadian grace? Painterly manner suits an Age of Elegance, as did that fascinating Pellegrini follower, Gian Antonio Guardi (elder brother of the famous landscape painter). In his flying *Cherubs* and dazzling *Aurora,* it is as if a sudden ray of sunlight had struck the painted surface, spreading slivers of color all around. Painterly painting at this point reaches a limit after which there will only remain the pseudo-scientific applications of Impressionism or Pointillism.

The painterly style however is detected in other Venetian masters in the Settecento, who generally are not associated with it. Although he drew very carefully from reality, with an exacting graphic technique, Pietro Longhi reached an unsurpassed *naïveté* and freshness when he used colors. Especially towards the end of his long career as a painter of conversation pieces (1740-1785), Longhi defined a gracious, ironic manner where the painterly touch is practically substituted for the structure of drawing.

It is even more interesting to note how much of the painterly touch of the major masters passed to such specialized "viewpainters" as Canaletto and Francesco Guardi. The former almost never made preparatory drawings for the hundreds of little figures *(macchiette)* which fill his lively views of Venice (and London). The few that do exist are like pure profile drawings, more to fix a detail than to catch an impression. But when Canaletto comes to paint the *Visit of the Doge* at the San Rocco, he creates a masterpiece in the painterly style. Swinging and agile, dotted and brilliant, Canaletto's brush creates his small world of characters, giving the most faithful portrait of his times. Naturally, the painterly principle is more evident in Canaletto's landscape drawings, especially those which are the free first ideas for future paintings. One sheet in Philadelphia, a view of the *Old Fish Market,* explains how the master could capture the breath of a passing cloud with his painterly stroke, which expresses all the immediate liveliness of a natural event.

Is Francesco Guardi also a painterly interpreter of the Venetian environment? A comparison between some of his drawings and the one we have just mentioned by Canaletto establishes a strong connecting link; actually the latter was called a good pupil, *"buon scolaro del Canaletto."* But the quality of Guardi's painterly manner is subtly different, emphasizing the basic human difference between the artists. Canaletto is a man of the Enlightenment; he never forgets a certain scientific realism. Francesco Guardi, on the contrary, embodies many of the qualities and anxieties of the future, from Romanticism to Impressionism. His Venetian views bear all the melancholy and frailty of the secret heart of a crumbling empire. His extreme, painterly touch—fractured, short and vibrating, like the changing surface of mother-of-pearl—leaves us with a sense of poignancy and loss. His paintings are sometimes like an ineffable lyrical utterance, wasted in a world which no longer listens.

By E. Haverkamp-Begemann

The Sketch

Its functions in the hands of three masters: Rubens, Rembrandt, Jan Brueghel

E. Haverkamp-Begemann is Chairman of the
Department of the History of Art at Yale and
an authority on seventeenth-century Dutch painting.

The Sketch

Three individuals, three different approaches to the oil sketch. Each used the medium for a different purpose, and valued the degree of finish differently. A comparison clarifies the nature and the role of the sketch in the work of each artist.

Let us begin by reviewing briefly the main categories of Rubens' sketches. First, there are those which served the artist to jot down an idea at an initial stage, such as the sketch of *St. Barbara Fleeing* in the Ashmolean Museum at Oxford. Filippo Baldinucci, recording in 1681 the seventeenth-century terminology in use by artists, would have called this and similar first ideas *"bozzetti"* or *"bozze"* which he defined as "small models or paintings, which the artists make as the beginning of their work in order to enlarge them later, in painting, in sculpture or in another medium." The term *bozzetto* was used for sketches collected by Cardinal Leopoldo de' Medici, in the inventory made of his collection in 1675 and the years following. Baldinucci reserved the term *"schizzi"* for drawings, in which sense Rubens also used the word.

A second category consists of oil sketches submitted to the patron for approval, the *"modelli."* In its finish and function, the *modello* is comparable to the *"vidimus"* which glass painters submitted for approval to their patrons. One example for a *modello* which on documentary evidence is known to have been submitted to patrons is the sketch of *Christ Carrying the Cross* in the Rijksmuseum, Amsterdam, which Rubens made as the *modello* for the painting in the Abbey of Afflighem and which he showed to the patrons in 1634. Almost all the details of the large painting are already present in this *modello*. While painting, Rubens changed details in this *modello*, for instance the figures at the bottom. It is very likely that a *modello* was often started as a *bozzetto*, and it cannot always be established whether a *bozzetto* was meant as such or whether it was intended to be carried further into the more highly developed *modello* stage.

A third category consists of sketches that Rubens made for his assistants as examples for the work to be carried out by them. These *"modelli* for artists" were made for painters, tapestry weavers, print-makers, sculptors, silversmiths and architects. An example is the

well-documented decoration for the Jesuit church in Antwerp. It was agreed that Rubens' assistants could be allowed to execute the paintings on the basis of the sketches if Rubens himself would retouch the final product. For some ceilings Rubens made first a quick study. The *St. Barbara Fleeing* at Oxford is such a *bozzetto*, drawn in brown and white lines only. It was followed by a larger, colored *modello* for the assistants (Dulwich) in which Rubens elaborated details and reduced the figures with regard to the space surrounding them. Rubens often amplified space and reduced detail while proceeding to greater finish, as has been observed by various writers.

The character of *"modelli* for artists" is often influenced by the nature of the work for which it was painted. *The Meeting of Abraham and Melchisedech* (National Gallery, Washington) is a case in point. The sketch is Rubens' final design immediately preceding the large canvas which was the direct model for the tapestry weaver. Architecture as well as figures, background, putti and all other elements are carefully formulated and fully defined. The sketch is distinguished by a preponderance of gold in the triglyphs of the architrave, in columns, vases, and in garlands decorating the plinth at the bottom of the composition. The gold was introduced for the tapestry weaver, and so was the clarity in outlines of figures, and in the separation of one form from another which should make it easy for the weaver to define figures and objects when translating them into tapestry.

The characteristics of many *modelli* depend on the medium for which they were made (print, sculpture, ivory or silver), and also on other factors like the dependability of those who were responsible for the execution of the final product. A greater degree of dependability allowed for a lower degree of finish of the *modello*, and vice-versa. Thus the sketch for the title page of M. C. Sarbievius, *Lyricorum Libri IV*, engraved by Cornelis Galle, is more freely executed and is not as linear as *Christ Carrying the Cross* in Berkeley's University Art Museum for the engraving by Paul Pontius. Both prints appeared in 1632, and we must assume that in one Rubens did not want to give the print-maker a chance for free interpretation, while in the other one he left details summarily indicated. Similar differences in finish can be observed between *modelli* belonging to one series, such as *The Life of Achilles*. The degree of finish in such instances may depend on whether the sketch

Central detail of Rembrandt's *St. John the Baptist Preaching*, ca. 1635 (about 1 1/2 times actual size). Staatliche Museen, Berlin.

Rubens' first sketch, or *bozzetto*, for *The Flight of St. Barbara* in the ceiling of the Jesuit Church, Antwerp, ca. 1620; brown grisaille with white accents on wood panel, 6 inches high. Ashmolean Museum, Oxford.

was an early one in the series to be "enlarged" by an assistant, or a late one.

Another reason for Rubens to refrain from further completion was the function of the sketch as a mere supplement to another one. Rubens' patrons agreed with the *modello* of *Christ Carrying the Cross* for the Abbey of Afflighem, but stipulated that Rubens should make the painting *"meliora forma,"* signifying "improved in shape" or "of a better format." Rubens had to rearrange the composition in order to make it fit the taller painting and painted a sketch which is now in the Royal Museum in Copenhagen. Details of figures, landscape and objects present in the Amsterdam *modello* were not repeated in the Copenhagen sketch, but were supposed to remain virtually the same. The impression of unfinishedness in the Copenhagen sketch, therefore, is misleading insofar as it is a partial definition of a much more fully developed work of art. It should not be considered unfinished, but should rather be thought of as one of two parts supplementing each other, and it can only properly be evaluated if seen in relation to the earlier but more nearly complete sketch.

Unlike Rubens, Rembrandt seems to have painted oil sketches only for etchings, not for paintings or other works of art. Rembrandt's earliest oil sketch for an etching is *Christ Presented to the People* of 1634 in the National Gallery in London. Rembrandt modeled the total composition in a few tones, namely yellowish-brown, grey and off-white, on a brownish ground, and the work may be called a sketch in *chiaroscuro*. It is the only sketch by Rembrandt which resembles Rubens' sketches for prints in purpose and characteristics. Probably following Rubens' example, Rembrandt painted a sketch for an etching which was largely executed by pupils, and the sketch was meant as a model for them.

Rembrandt made sketches for other etchings as an aid to himself. This use of the oil sketch in preparation for etchings was unprecedented. It can be explained only in the context of Rembrandt's etching style which was equally novel. Endeavoring to create painterly etchings, Rembrandt was forced to work on the copper plate in a manner which was the opposite of painting in oils on canvas or panel: instead of modeling primarily with light tones on a dark background as in painting, he had to draw those areas on the red copper plate that would print dark and leave the plate blank for the highlights.

In order to facilitate modeling with dark areas, he thus established the composition first in the traditional way of the painter, that is by modeling primarily in light tones. In this manner he painted the final representation of a subject of which the details had already been established. These sketches, therefore, do not mark the beginning of a creative process; neither are they examples for others, but they are rather the last step before the final realization of the etchings. *Joseph Telling His Dreams* in the Rijksmuseum illustrates this point. It is much closer to the etching than the three

drawings which preceded the sketch. By the time Rembrandt painted the sketch most of the compositional problems had been ironed out, and the etching differs only in details of minor importance from the oil sketch. Similar is the function of the oil sketch, also in the Rijksmuseum, which Rembrandt painted for the etched *Portrait of Dr. Ephraim Bueno* (H. 226). Rembrandt did not search for pose or facial expression but for chiaroscuro. The painted light tones carry the composition, while part of the background at the right consists of the untouched reddish brown color of the paper (pasted on wood) on which Rembrandt painted

Rubens' larger colored *modello* of *The Flight of St. Barbara*, intended as a guide for his assistants. Panel, 12 1/2 inches high. Dulwich College, London.

Rubens' grisaille sketch, *Christ Carrying the Cross,* for an engraving, 1632. Univ. of California, Berkeley.

Rubens modified the format in his later sketch for the Affli-ghem altarpiece, 1636, 40 1/2 inches high. Copenhagen Museum.

Christ Carrying the Cross, the *modello* Rubens presented to his patrons in 1634, 28 7/8 inches high. Rijksmuseum, Amsterdam.

In his oil sketch for the titlepage of Sarbievius' *Lyricorum Libri IV*, 1632, Rubens left considerable freedom of interpretation to his engraver, the outstanding Antwerp print-maker, Cornelis Galle. Museum Plantijn Moretus, Antwerp.

Rembrandt's earliest known oil sketch for an etching, *Christ Presented to the People*, 1634,
21 3/8 inches high, yellowish brown, grey and off-white. National Gallery, London.

the sketch; in the etching the background would have to be etched, and the white of the paper would serve for the highlights.

There can hardly be any doubt that *The Concord of the State* was also painted for an etching. The main difference between this and the oil sketches already mentioned is the greater transparency of the dark areas. We should not forget, however, that Rembrandt's style of etching in 1641 also differed markedly from that of the years 1634-35, and that the greater transparency of the dark areas is one of the most characteristic differences between these and earlier etchings. If we could translate *The Concord of the State* into an etching we probably would end up with one similar in style to such etchings of 1641 as *The Presentation in the Temple* or the "small" *Raising of Lazarus*. At this stage of

preparing the etching Rembrandt apparently had mainly doubts about the space at the bottom, and added a strip after he had completed most of the rest. Almost the entire sketch has been defined without many changes, which is surprising for such a highly complicated program. It remains a mystery why the etching was not executed.

The *Preaching of St. John the Baptist* in Berlin is similar to *The Concord of the State* in many respects. Rembrandt enlarged the original small canvas at the time of its execution with a narrow strip at the right, and probably sometime later he added more canvas all around. In the general aspect of brushwork, in the application of highlights and other details the sketch resembles that of *The Concord of the State*, and it may also have been made with an etching in mind. For the

Rembrandt's little *Portrait of the Jewish Physician Ephraim Bueno,* 7 1/2 inches high (left; Rijksmuseum, Amsterdam) was a study in chiaroscuro for the etching (above), dated 1647.

Rubens' highly finished modello, *The Meeting of Abraham and Melchisedech*, ca. 1625, 26 inches hi is the final design preceding the large canvas for one of the series of tapestries commissioned by the Infanta Isabella on the theme of "The Triumph of the Eucharist." National Gallery, Washington, D

Rubens' *Study of a Head*,
ca. 1600-10. Galleria Nazionale, Rome.

Rubens' *Adoration of the Magi*, ca. 1609-10, 136 1/4 inches high. Prado Museum.
The head of the kneeling king is evidently based on the oil study above.

Undoubtedly a *modello* for an etching, Rembrandt's *The Concord of State*, 1641, 29 inches high, is a visualization of the printed image. Boymans Museum, Rotterdam.

Rembrandt's *St. John the Baptist Preaching*, ca. 1635, 24 inches high, probably also was a sketch for an etching (see detail page 58). Staatliche Museen, Berlin.

time being, however, it seems more prudent to leave the question open.

Although Rembrandt's oil sketches for works of art which were executed were all painted for etchings, not all of them were made at a late stage in the development of the composition. There is one exception, namely *The Lamentation over Christ,* in the National Gallery in London, which is connected with two etchings, the *Crucifixion* (small plate, H. 123) and *Christ Crucified between Two Thieves* (H. 173). The sketch, therefore, was probably made with an etching in mind, but the final form of the etching differed considerably from it. A part of this sketch was preceded by a drawing, now in the British Museum. It has the same stylistic characteristics as the oil sketch and is composed of a large number of pieces of paper, cut and pasted together, and drawn with pen, chalk, brush and even oil. If the oil sketch was made for an etching, the drawing was too, and in that case Rembrandt prepared the light-dark values of etchings in another medium than oil.

If this is so, the elaborately finished drawing *Christ Speaking to His Disciples* (Haarlem), done with the brush over red and black chalk, and which has its closest parallels in the London drawing, perhaps should also be considered as a design for an etching. The drawing may have been the first idea for what finally, more than ten years later, was going to be the *Hundred Guilder Print.* In subject-matter the drawing and the print are closely related, and whatever the final identification of the subject of the drawing might be, it is similar to that of

Rembrandt's *Lamentation over the Dead Christ,* ca. 1642, 13 inches high. National Gallery, London.

The first state of Rembrandt's *Christ between Two Thieves,* one of two etchings connected with *The Lamentation* (left).

With primary accent on lights and shadows, Rembrandt's
almost completely monochrome painting, *Joseph
Telling His Dreams*, ca. 1636-37, 20 inches high,
is close to the last step before his etching
of the subject (right). Rijksmuseum, Amsterdam.

Christ Speaking to His Disciples, 1634, brush
over red and black chalk. Teyler Museum, Haarlem.

Rembrandt: *Joseph Telling His Dreams,*
etching, 1638, 4 inches high.

Rembrandt's famous etching, *Christ Healing
the Sick,* the "Hundred Guilder Print," ca. 1649,
was probably derived from his large
drawing (top) done more than 10 years earlier.

the etching. Given the similarity in subject-matter of the drawing and the print, and in the technique of the drawing and the sketches for etchings, it seems certainly possible that Rembrandt made the large drawing as a design for an etching which finally developed into the *Hundred Guilder Print.*

Apparently Rembrandt did not paint *bozzetti* as Rubens did, and did not use the oil sketch to give initial form to an idea for a painting or etching. For first formulations he made drawings, or used the canvas or panel on which the painting was to be executed. The painting itself was the *bozzetto* before it was completed, and often remained a *bozzetto* even after Rembrandt had decided that it was finished. Rembrandt expressed himself fully in the unfinished, fragmentary and variable state of a work of art. Most of the numerous drawings of religious scenes are finished in their sketchiness; the broad brushstrokes in paintings that leave the forms undefined, and the dark areas in etchings which conceal and obscure more than they reveal, are the perfect expression of Rembrandt's intentions. Paradoxically, therefore, the *"non finito"* is more pronounced in these finished works than in some of his oil sketches which mainly served one specific purpose.

The unfinished and the sketchy were goals for Rembrandt, while for Rubens they were steps towards completion of a work of art. There is another difference in this respect between the two artists. Rembrandt frequently painted heads or busts in a sketchy way from nature, after other persons or after himself; Rubens did

Sketching from nature: Jan Brueghel the Elder's *Donkeys, Monkeys and Other Animals,*
from which the monkeys were used as a detail in his *Paradise.* Kunsthistorisches Museum, Vienna.

Rubens: *Negro Head*, ca. 1618, 18 inches high. Hyde Collection, Glens Falls, N.Y.

Jan Brueghel the Elder: *Dogs*.
Kunsthistorisches Museum, Vienna.

so only rarely. Rembrandt painted such oil studies from nature as character studies of individuals while Rubens painted heads with greater finish in an effort to create types. He then used these types in certain roles in his paintings. An example is the *Study of a Head* in the Galleria Nazionale, Rome, recurring as the head of the kneeling king in the sketch of the *Adoration of the Magi* in the Groningen Museum and in the corresponding painting in the Prado. Similar facial characteristics are found in a number of oil studies (Metropolitan Museum, New York; Lord Belper; Leningrad; and elsewhere) and in drawings. The highly stylized hair and features in the oil study in Rome and in many similar paintings are part of the type created by Rubens, rather than features of models.

Drawing from nature, primarily for the sake of recording it, is found only occasionally in Rubens' sketches. One of the few instances is the sketch of *Negro Heads* in Brussels, at least if these studies can be accepted as a work of Rubens; another is the sketch of a *Negro Head* in the Louis F. Hyde Collection, Glens Falls, N.Y.

This type of sketch from nature probably was created by Jan Brueghel. His sketches of animals, one of *Dogs*, the other one of *Donkeys, Monkeys and other Animals* (in the Kunsthistorisches Museum, Vienna) are studies from nature made to record these creatures in various attitudes so that he could study them for his paintings. In 1912 Gustav Glück had recognized that the monkeys were studies by Jan Brueghel for his *Paradise* in The Hague.

Later, a sketch of *Negroes and a Muscovite* in the Harrach'sche Gemäldegalerie, Vienna, was also correctly attributed to Jan Brueghel (by Günther Heinz), and it was deduced that one must have been painted before 1609 because some heads are also found in Rubens' *Adoration of the Magi* of that year (before Rubens repainted it, almost 20 years later). Jan Brueghel's way of preparing the panel for the sketch is similar to that of Rubens, and it is likely that Rubens adopted from the elder artist both some technical procedures and the type of the sketched study of exotic heads.

Painting heads was for Rubens primarily a matter of invention. In that respect he was still under the spell of sixteenth-century artistic theories. Once painting studies of human heads from nature had been established as an acceptable practice, it was taken up rapidly by other artists. Both van Dyck and Jordaens painted such studies of heads which they later included in paintings, but in Flanders the recording of exotic heads preceded the depiction of the readily available model. In Holland, Rembrandt went his own way, and sketched heads in oil from nature in his lifelong pursuit of man's psyche.

In conclusion, it seems therefore that Jan Brueghel, Rubens and Rembrandt used the same medium for their own purposes, and achieved different effects that suited their respective aims and temperaments. Rubens rarely sketched heads from nature, and in cases where he did so, the practice came to him from Jan Brueghel. Rembrandt, who found in sketchiness, in the *non finito,* the perfect means of expression, used the medium of the oil sketch in preparation for etchings mainly for one specific purpose—to establish the proper relationship between light and dark shapes. The characteristics of Rubens' sketches depend to some extent on the purpose for which they were painted and on the circumstances inherent to their use. We thus must be aware of the possibility that the sketch in its completeness does not necessarily correspond with an equally incomplete idea. Oil sketches cannot properly be evaluated unless they are seen in close connection with the other elements of the creative process to which they belong.

The present essay is a revised and somewhat abbreviated version of the writer's "Purpose and Style: Oil Sketches of Rubens, Jan Brueghel, Rembrandt" which appeared in *Stil und Überlieferung in der Kunst des Abendlandes,* III, Berlin (Gebrüder Mann) 1967, pp. 104-113. In some instances the writer's opinions here differ from those expressed in the earlier version. For Bibliography, see the earlier publication.

By Francis Watson

Fragonard

Painterly and non-painterly in the France of Louis XVI

Francis Watson is Director of the Wallace Collection,
London, and the author of a two-volume
publication on the Wrightsman Collection, New York.

Fragonard

From the beginning Fragonard had one of the stigmata of the painterly painter. For him, painting itself was an ineluctable activity; he had to be painting or drawing all the time. The creative urge to use his brush welled up in him like a force of nature which he could not resist. When his father made him a lawyer's clerk in Paris, his master, the notary, noticed that he was forever drawing caricatures in the margins of his law books. It was he, not Fragonard's father, the unsuccessful haberdasher's assistant, who suggested that the young Jean-Honoré—he was only between 14 and 15 years old at the time—should be apprenticed to an artist, for the law was clearly not his *métier*.

Fragonard became the most prolific of artists. The late Georges Wildenstein includes just short of 550 items in the *catalogue raisonné* of the artist's paintings and his list unquestionably errs in the direction of conservatism. In the first two of the three volumes in which he is cataloguing all Fragonard's drawings, M. Ananof lists some 1,400 surviving drawings from Fragonard's hand but acknowledges that at least 1,000 more dating from the artist's first visit to Italy alone are missing today.

Such activity is prodigious. Even while Fragonard was still a student, contemporary critics spoke of his "astounding facility." Natoire, the head of the Académie Française at Rome, where Fragonard was sent after winning a Prix de Rome scholarship, reported to the Marquis de Marigny, *Directeur des Bâtiments,* that "there is no reason to fear that Fragonard will damp the fire that is his great gift from nature." He added, "I see things he has done which give me great hope for his future." It was a far-sighted prophecy. Fragonard was, in fact, a born painter with a spirit that was all fire and air.

The range of his work matches its profuseness; it includes history and religious paintings, genre, scenes of domestic life, *fêtes galantes,* landscapes, portraits and copies after old masters. Only tragic or sad subjects are absent from his oeuvre; or dull ones like still-life. They were foreign to his sunny Provençal nature (he was born at Grasse). Such a wealth of output suggests that Fragonard was a rapid worker, another mark of the painterly painter, and such was indeed the case. On the back of the canvas of one of his most spontaneous

The liquid color seems almost floated on: *A Young Scholar,* ca. 1773, 17 inches high. Wallace Collection, London.

portraits, the *Monseur de la Bretèche* in the Louvre, a contemporary, possibly the sitter himself, has written *"Portrait de la Bretèche, peint par Fragonard en 1769, en une heure de temps."* (Portrait of de la Bretèche painted by Fragonard in 1769 in the space of a single hour.) The canvas is a large one. The sitter is shown life-size, in Spanish costume, seated in three-quarter length playing a mandolin or guitar. The painter has quite clearly attacked his task with the highest excitement. The paint is liquid and seems to have flowed from his brush onto the canvas with all the ease of a fountain playing or a spring bubbling up from the earth. Not for a moment has he hesitated. There are no changes of composition or *pentimenti.* The artist's technical skill, his intellect and his feelings are concentrated exactly at the tip of his brush.

This happy facility was an inborn characteristic and certainly was not learned from his masters. When it was decided that Fragonard should become a painter, his mother, with great perspicacity, took him straight to François Boucher, one of the greatest French artists of the eighteenth century, and indeed of all time. Boucher, however, refused to accept a young and entirely untrained boy into his studio. He was, after all, the leading painter of the day and can hardly be blamed for this. Instead, he suggested sending Jean-Honoré to learn how to handle paint from Chardin, another very distinguished painter but of a quite different sort from Boucher. Chardin was one of the greatest technicians of the day. His still-lifes are miracles of painting, of the actual laying of the paint on the canvas. But his methods were slow, careful and profoundly meditated. *"On cherche, on frotte, on glace"* ("You search, you scumble, you glaze"), he said. Such methods were at the opposite pole to Fragonard's natural style. Such teaching did not interest him. Nor did the still-life paintings which were Chardin's specialty. But at least he learned from Chardin how to set his palette and manipulate his brushes. So when he returned once again to Boucher, the great Court painter consented to take him into his studio through which some of the most brilliant painters of the day had passed.

Now Boucher, in spite of the very real qualities which made him one of the greatest French painters of his century, was not a painterly painter. He was above all a draftsman. The vast number of his drawings which survive bear witness to this, and it is confirmed by the brief glimpses we get of his methods of teaching in Mannlich's.

memoirs. Boucher's pupils were thoroughly grounded in academic drawing, especially drawing of the nude, and many of the best of these he signed himself as a mark of approbation. He composed with a great sense of the decorative and painted with great facility but in a highly artificial, somewhat tightly handled style, with a restricted range of colors of great brilliance and vividness. For this color scheme, as we know, he drew inspiration from his prized collection of blue butterflies and his mineralogical collection. Thus his colors were not related directly to observation of his subjects.

But what Boucher taught Fragonard was very important even if his influence on the younger artist's actual manner of handling paint was the least significant aspect of it. First and foremost he inspired him with a delight in the old masters that he had loved himself, especially G.B. Tiepolo, Rubens and Rembrandt, all of whom were

to influence Fragonard profoundly. Boucher obtained for him access to the great private collections of Paris such as those of Pierre Crozat and the Comte de Vence where he could see and study their works. Among the earliest of Fragonard's recorded works are a number of copies after Rembrandt as well as after other Flemish and Dutch masters. His acquaintance with Tiepolo was to bear fruit when he visited Venice with the Abbé de Saint-Non a few years later in 1760; there he did numerous drawings after Tiepolo's frescoes. To understand fully what the younger artist learned from his master it is necessary to consider what Boucher was producing in the years from about 1748 to 1752 when Jean-Honoré was working in his studio. The older painter, 45 and at the height of his powers, was engaged on a series of pastoral subjects and scenes from classical mythology for the various royal palaces. In the year

Portrait of Fragonard's friend and patron, *Abbé de Saint-Non in Spanish Costume,* ca. 1769, 36 5/8 inches high. Barcelona Museum.

Portrait of M. de la Bretèche (brother of the Abbé de Saint-Non), 1769, inscribed "painted in an hour." Louvre.

ne of some 20 of Fragonard's *"portraits de fantaisie": The Warrior*, ca. 1769,
1 1/2 inches high. Clark Art Institute, Williamstown, Mass.

Fragonard as a pupil of Boucher: *The Musical Contest,*
ca. 1750, 27 1/2 inches high. Wallace Collection, London.

Boucher: *A Summer Pastoral,*
1749. Wallace Collection.

Fragonard: *Blindman's Buff,*
ca. 1750. Toledo (O.) Museum.

But into his works produced under the immediate inspiration of Boucher, Fragonard introduced essential differences of handling from his master's manner. This is apparent from the very beginning of his career in such works as the small canvases of the *Musical Contest* in the Wallace Collection which is actually signed F.B. (for Francois Boucher) and was almost certainly produced while Frago was working as a pupil in Boucher's studio. It is still more evident in works like *La Jardinière (The Lady Gardener)* in Lady Beaverbrook's collection or *Blind Man's Buff (Le Colin Maillard)* in the Toledo Museum, probably painted towards the middle of the 1750s. The subjects and compositions derive directly from Boucher, but the younger artist departs from his master's color scheme almost entirely. Instead of the cold bluish greens and pale daffodil yellows of Boucher's landscape backgrounds there is a new warmth of color and the costumes and flesh colors are warmer too; strong reds, bright yellows and blues predominate. This warmth and a new note of humane feeling come out strongly in the actual handling of the paint, loose and fluid, where Boucher's is often tight and brittle.

To appreciate to the full what Fragonard made of Boucher's style we must consider a painting like *Rinaldo in the Garden of Armida,* painted soon after his return from Italy. Here the subject is a completely Boucher one; so is the composition, except that a new sense of movement and vitality, foreign to Boucher, has been introduced. But it is in the actual handling of the paint that the differences are most striking. The touch is far more broken than Boucher ever permitted himself. Every stroke of the brush tells and is instinct with vitality. The spectator can follow and almost repeat in his imagination the motions of the artist's hand as he excitedly dashed the paint onto the canvas.

Of course Fragonard did not always paint with quite this vitality. In what is perhaps his most celebrated though not, in my view, his finest painting, *Les Hasards Heureux de l'Escarpolette (The Swing),* in the Wallace Collection, Frago comes very close indeed to Boucher's handling—especially in the pale refined greeny-blue broccoli of the massed foliage in the background. The overtly erotic nature of the subject matter, the fact that it was ordered by the *Receveur-général des biens du Clergé,* a certain baron Saint-Julien, who first approached the religious painter Doyen to carry out the unsuitable commission, all combined to give it just that salty anecdotal quality which established its high reputa-

after Fragonard left him he completed his two greatest masterpieces of decoration, the *Rising* and the *Setting of the Sun,* huge canvases intended as models for tapestry weaving at the Gobelins factory; he himself considered these to be his supreme achievements and he must have begun them while Fragonard was still in the studio. He was also painting landscapes *"dans le style de Benedetto,"* i.e. of Castiglione. All these types of painting Fragonard was to adopt and make his own, though he only once worked on anything like the scale required for the decoration of the royal palaces—in the decorations for Louveciennes rejected by Mme. du Barry and presently in the Frick Collection, New York.

Rembrandt's *The Holy Family with Angels*, 1645,
45 5/8 inches high. Hermitage, Leningrad.

Fragonard's *The Holy Family with Angels, after Rembrandt,*
ca. 1748-52, 35 1/2 inches high. Private collection.

Rubens: *The Consequences of War*, ca. 1637-38,
81 inches high. Pitti Palace, Florence.

Fragonard: Drawing after Rubens' *The Consequences of War*,
black crayon, 6 3/4 inches high. British Museum, London.

tion in the nineteenth century. But today it seems to
hint that the artist was hardly at ease with the
commission. The stiff handling, the conventional color
scheme, everything seems to isolate it as far as possible
from the real world by a sort of moral *cordon sanitaire,*
as though he found the subject matter distasteful. The
same handling, deriving directly from Boucher's manner
of painting, is to be found in the later *Fête at
Rambouillet* (Lisbon, Gulbenkian Foundation) where a
dream-like setting is certainly intended.

Here it may be desirable to clear away the popular
idea that Fragonard was a painter of erotic subjects and
suggestive boudoir scenes. He painted a few, of course,
but the fact that he withdrew *La Baigneuse* and its
pendant, essays in the manner of his master Boucher,
from the Salon of 1767 *"en raison de sa délicatesse trop
scrupuleuse"* (by reason of his over-scrupulous delicacy)
suggests that he was uninterested in the pornographic.
Even Cochin, who rebuked him for "devoting himself to
works scarcely in keeping with his genius," admitted
that he was compelled to do this by the Crown's failure
to pay for commissioned works and when it finally paid,
paying really far too little. When Fragonard did produce
his rare scenes of passion, such as the famous *Le Feu*

Fragonard: *The New Model*, ca. 1770,
20 inches high. Musée Jacquemart-André, Paris.

aux Poudres (All Ablaze; Louvre), the lost *La Gimblette (The Ring Biscuit),* the series of *Kisses* or *La Chemise Enlevée (The Stolen Shift;* Louvre), they are emptied of any overt suggestiveness by their brilliant and spirited handling. This is particularly noticeable in the last of these where the vivacious treatment of the subject is echoed in the vivacity of the brushwork by which the thin, liquid color seems almost to be floated onto the surface of the canvas with something of the brilliance of Rubens' sketches.

It was in the years immediately following his return from Rome in the spring of 1761 that Fragonard really began to display to the full his virtuoso brilliance in

handling paint. This is perhaps best seen in two separate groups of paintings executed a few years apart. After beginning on a number of landscapes based on drawings he had made in company with Hubert Robert in Italy he painted a large series of *Têtes d'Expression,* heads of old men, in no sense portraits. These were inspired partly by the similar "imaginary" or "fancy" portraits he must have found Tiepolo executing when he visited Venice, but also influenced by Baroccio and Guercino with whose work he came into contact during his Italian travels. Rembrandt, too, with whom he had become familiar when studying private collections in Paris, made a contribution to these imaginative creations, especially

Fragonard's *The Stolen Shift*, ca. 1765-67,
14 inches high. Louvre Museum, Paris

the late Rembrandt with his broadly brushed manner. About 20 of these heads survive out of a much larger number probably commissioned by the Paris dealer Emmanuel de Ghendt. Akin to them but painted a few years later in the second half of the 1760s and early 1770s is a series of *portraits de fantaisie*, in which real men are represented, but in which facial expression is stressed less than a certain element of fantasy in the costume—a sort of compromise between the male costume of the Henri III period and the female costume of Henri IV's time with a certain added Spanish element. This last derives from Carl van Loo's *Spanish Conversation* (commissioned by the blue-stocking Mme.

Geoffrin), which enjoyed a great vogue during this particular period.

Both these series show the artist's painterly virtuosity at its highest point. The paint in the heads of old men comes very close to Rubens' handling at its loosest and most vigorous and, with its broad flowing brush-strokes, looks forward to the late nineteenth century in brilliance of coloring. Like these, the *portraits de fantaisie* (one of the best is the portrait of the artist's friend and patron, the Abbé de Saint-Non) were clearly painted in the heat of emotion and at great speed. The case of the Bretèche portrait, painted within an hour, has already been mentioned; and on the reverse of another of the series Fragonard himself recorded that it was completed in a mere half-hour.

In their boldness of presentation certain of these *portraits de fantaisie* recall the work of Frans Hals. This is not entirely surprising, for the artist undertook a journey into the Low Countries with Bergeret de Grancourt, the *fermier-général* friend of his Italian travels, at an uncertain date, probably in the early 1770s. This resulted in a large number of drawings after masters like Rubens, van Dyck, Hals, Jordaens, etc. and awakened his interest in Netherlandish painting. His fondness for Dutch landscape had already emerged in a rather curious and unfamiliar form some six or seven years earlier—a series of landscapes in the manner of Ruisdael and Hobbema. A number of these are known and many more are recorded but remain untraced. It seems likely that they remain forgotten beneath discolored varnish under the generic description "School of Ruisdael." They are not particularly painterly in character. It is only in the figures that Fragonard's distinctive and vital brushwork appears, betraying the fact that they are his work and not merely the productions of the brush of some minor Dutch landscape painter of the seventeenth century. Fragonard would have become familiar with Dutch landscape painting in French collections long before his visit to the Low Countries; Dutch painting was as much the fashion in mid-eighteenth century Paris as Post-Impressionist painting has been in mid-twentieth century New York.

Fragonard's tour of Holland does not seem to have

The Watering-place, after Ruysdael, bistre wash, 9 3/4 inches high. British Museum, London.

Shepherd in a Landscape, or *The Herdsman*, ca. 1761, 14 7/8 inches high. Coll. Mr. & Mrs. O. Roy Chalk, New York.

Scene of domestic life: *The Schoolmistress*, or *Say Please*, ca. 1777-79, 10 7/8 inches high. Wallace Collection.

Detail from Fragonard's celebrated *The Swing*, 1766—the slightly erotic subject was commissioned by the Baron de Saint-Julien. Wallace Collection.

In the manner of Boucher: *The Lady Gardener*, ca. 1750. Coll. Lady Beaverbrook, Surrey.

Study of expression: *St. Jerome Reading*, ca. 1763, 22 1/4 inches high. Coll. D. David-Weill, Paris.

had any striking or immediate effect on his painting. This came rather later. Shortly after his return, the artist and his wife set off in October 1773 for a 12-month visit to Italy, traveling once again with Bergeret de Grancourt. This led to a second remarkable series of Italianate landscapes, painted on his return. But the voyage to the Netherlands certainly reawakened his interest in Rubens and in Dutch painting that bore very obvious fruit in the long series of scenes of domestic and family life which preoccupied him in the 1780s.

Except for Greuze, no painter of any eminence was so closely associated as Fragonard with the great revolution of morality and sentiment brought about by Rousseau's writings with their new emphasis on the virtues of domesticity and family life. If Greuze chiefly drew his subject-matter from the sentimental plays of Sedaine and other authors of the so-called *comédies larmoyantes* which enjoyed such a success in the 1750s and '60s, Frago's genre scenes of domestic life were clearly linked with the less grossly emotional novels which extolled the virtues of the "natural" life. His *Happy Family,* of which he painted two versions, is taken straight from Saint-Lambert's novel *Sara Th.,* in which a wealthy girl of good family marries a virtuous footman and retires to an arcadian life of idyllic poverty in the country. The mere titles of the paintings of these years—*L'Education fait Tout (Upbringing Is Everything;* São Paulo), *Le Petit Prédicateur (The Little Preacher;* Viel-Picard), *La Visite à la Nourrice (The Visit to the Foster Mother;* Washington, D.C.), *Dites donc: s'il vous plait (The Schoolmistress;* Wallace Collection) reveal their subject matter immediately. One and all, they derive their inspiration from Berquin's 60 volumes of moral tales of a Rousseauist character in which children play a leading role. Known as *L'Ami des Enfants,* this enormous work which began to appear in 1774 provided immensely popular reading, and gave a new word to the French language, *berquinade,* meaning works of an agreeable and somewhat insipid character inspired by the life of children.

But if Berquin's book and Dutch genre paintings provided the anecdotal inspiration for this group of Fragonard's works, their visual inspiration came from Rubens. The warm coloring—golden yellows, burnt sienas and umbers—the almost post-box reds, with occasional touches of green or blue, often floated on as thin glazes, are redolent of Rubens' technique. So is the fluent, turbulent brush work with its absolute certainty

of touch. Diderot's comment on a painting which Fragonard exhibited in the Salon of 1767 seems appropriate here: *"Belle omelette, bien douillette, bien jaune et bien brûlée"* ("An excellent omelette, nice and soft, very yellow and well-browned").

Frago was really a Rococo painter born a little too late. Even before he had returned from his student years in Italy the Neo-Classic movement was being launched both in the Rome he was quitting and the Paris to which he was returning. But for many years he remained untouched by this new orientation of taste and feeling. The *fêtes galantes* which were such a favorite subject for the artist were the archetypal subjects of the French Rococo. Fragonard was still painting such great canvases as *La Main Chaude (Game of Hot Cockles)* and *Le Cheval Fondu (Game of Horse and Rider;* both in the National Gallery, Washington) in the second half of the

Romantic allegory: *Fountain of Love,* ca. 1780, 24 inches high. Wallace Collection.

The Stolen Kiss, ca. 1760.
Hermitage, Leningrad.

In Frago's late, Neo-Classic style: *The Stolen Kiss,*
ca. 1785, 25 inches high. Hermitage, Leningrad.

Self-Portrait, ca. 1780. Palace of
the Legion of Honor, San Francisco.

1770s when the Neo-Classic style was fully established in Paris.

But by the middle of the next decade, or even a little earlier, marked signs of the effect of Neo-Classicism begin to appear in the painter's work. A certain frigidity is perceptible in a group of allegories with more or less classical subjects produced during these years. The earliest of them, *The Awakening of Nature,* was destroyed during the last war but is known by an engraving issued in 1780. In it, the Elements, borne by *putti,* pay homage at the foot of an austerely classical statue. His *Sacrifice to Love* is similar in its subject matter.

About five years later is *The Fountain of Love* (Wallace Collection), perhaps the best known of this group. The subject is treated in a markedly classical style and the paint, although it retains the colors of Diderot's "well-browned omelette" is handled in a much less free and painterly manner. The tiny *La Lettre* (also Wallace Collection) which today hangs close beside it and was engraved two years later is even more tightly handled (partly no doubt on account of its small size). It looks forward curiously to the Victorian age in its "Keepsake" sentiment. With *Le Baiser à La Dérobée (The Stolen Kiss)* at Leningrad (engraved in 1788) and one or two cognate works like *The Bolt* and *The Contract,* an altogether new type of paint handling is found. It derives from the smooth, almost metallic treatment, found in Dutch seventeenth-century genre scenes. In these, the limpid, highly finished treatment of the dresses, often of satin, and the furniture and other appurtenances, recall the paintings of Terborch, whom Frago's younger contemporary Boilly was just beginning to imitate with considerable popular success. Possibly such work was an attempt to meet criticisms which were being voiced at this time that his recent work did not show sufficient variety of drapery.

Fortunately these concessions to Neo-Classic taste did not mean that the artist had lost his original talent for spontaneity of handling. Now that his circumstances were easier than they had been, he was able to paint to please himself—not merely the public and the critics—and in the last years before the Revolution he executed a number of portraits of children, especially of his young son Evariste. In these all the old facility reappears and in such a portrait as the so-called *Young Scholar* (Wallace Collection) or the better-known *Portrait of a Boy Dressed as Pierrot* (Wallace Collection) the freshness of handling, the broken touch and the brilliance of the color come near to anticipating the early Renoir. Indeed after the opening of the Salle Lacaze at the Louvre in 1869, when Dr. Lacaze's Fragonards, amounting to nearly a dozen, first made it possible to study his work properly in a Parisian public gallery, Fragonard exercised great influence on the Impressionists. Renoir acknowledged openly that he was trying to emulate the great eighteenth-century master and that surely is a high tribute to Fragonard's qualities as a painterly painter. But it must not be forgotten that even more than a painterly painter, Fragonard was a great poet. His best epitaph is the felicitous words written by the Goncourts in the opening and closing sentences of their essay on the artist first published in 1865. At the beginning they write: *"Les poètes manquent au siècle dernier...(les) deux seuls poètes ont été deux peintres: Watteau et Fragonard"* (There was a lack of poets in the past century...the only ones were two painters: Watteau and Fragonard). In their final sentence they describe the great artist as *"le dernier feu de joie du dix-huitième siècle"* (the last bonfire of the eighteenth century).

By Rodrigo Moynihan

Constable

The discovery of how to paint from nature in nineteenth-century England

Rodrigo Moynihan, well-known English painter, has
published a book on Goya and more recently an article
on Eakins in ARTnews; he lives in the south of France.

Constable

Looking at a typical Constable one feels an underlying sense of difficulty and doubt. A sense of strain, a feeling that some element of "goodness" had, on the limited surface of his canvas, finally eluded the painter. The vast sky moves restlessly over the solid intricacies of earth; the flickering touch and overlaid impasto explain and insist. An effect is captured but was this the essence? The drive to final realization seemed endless, a pilgrimage through a jungle maze.

Constable professed a pious affection for Nature but was not deeply moved by its sublime or grandiose aspects; it was the nature of a place with its specific differences and moods which dominated his imagination; moreover, the subject of the painting contained not only trees, meadows and clouds, but the ghosts of Rembrandt, Ruysdael and Claude. He and Delacroix were different in many fundamental respects, but both shared an obsessional interest in pictures and in the stylistic sources of their art. If it took a long time for style to mature, very early on he formed strict limits to the area of his interest. Turner's titles are great generalizations: *A Frosty Morning, Storm over the Alps, Fire at Sea;* Constable's flatly describe the name of the place. His plea that there was room for "a natural painter" was more an assertion for painting rather than poeticizing, although he knew well enough that his vision could only in the end impose itself by feeling. He had to evolve a style which could both serve movement and at the same time insist on permanence. Again and again he states the alternatives: trapping the movement of light and air in a butterfly net or, as he himself said, "driving the nail in deeper and deeper." The temptation to be resisted was tinging reality with a false emotional hue; a layer of sentiment corrupting the air of the painting. Yet, in his finest work—like *The Cenotaph*—this sentiment is built into the paint, strengthening the power of the image. It is impossible to look at a Constable without taking into account the nature of this poetic feeling and how it fails when floating gauchely over the painting.

Constable was an early example of a new kind of artist. The kind to which no great talent has been given as a natural right. Character is the cradle. There ideas are born, and the necessity, the will to follow great examples, and to make a credo of what is possible for yourself to do. The artist creates the artist and to this end must have a clear and obstinate notion of what art should be. The Truth must be found: by experiment, elimination and sacrifice; from it develops "his limited and abstracted art." Poetry is seeing the limited objective in a certain way, not a modest aim for Constable who, at heart, was interested only in the greatness of art. Like Cézanne his aim was to prove *"la petite sensation"* as a veritable source in its making.

The tensions in Cézanne's and Constable's lives show many similarities. Both were heavily handicapped by a lack of facility and dependent on successful, domineering fathers. It was within a confined space, the bounds of family life and understanding, that they strove to prove themselves. Progress would be slow and within a strict framework of self-imposed discipline but, eventually, the symbolic parental blessing might be given. There is a sense of divine authority brooding over East Bergholt and Aix, erecting the Tablets in the Garden of Eden, and commanding the rebellious artist to order. In spite of breaking rules they knew to be wrong, their deep desire was for official approval. When this was withheld they both suffered from the same kind of paranoia and sense of betrayal. Deeply conservative, politically and socially, they suspected honors considered not quite right or emanating from the wrong quarter. Constable was strangely unmoved by French recognition, as Cézanne by the enthusiasm of young painters. The seal of success to them was the accolade of Academy or Salon, and it was bitterly resented when not forthcoming. Failure was underlined when close friends and admirers were patronizing or joined a note of anxiety to their encouragement.

The grudging respect accorded to Constable may have been due to the very qualities of his character. Goodness rather than brilliance, and goodness apt to change too abruptly to cattiness and bad temper. For, of course, he did feel misunderstood. His working life coincided with a great upsurge of painting in England; landscape, though still considered a lesser art, had been made respectable by the work of Wilson, Gainsborough, Crome and Cozens. All the characteristics of the English School had been defined; freshness of color, spontaneity of handling, Romantic informality. Reynolds, followed by Lawrence, had already made paint itself look different. There was a narrower area between oil painting and watercolor. By 1815 Turner had already

Detail of *The Hay Wain*, 1821 (National Gallery, London), shows the specificity of Constable's direct approach to nature.

Claude made the landscape a respectable, if still a lesser, subject for the English:
Landscape with Mercury and the Shepherd Battus, ca. 1662 (Chatsworth Settlement).

Salomon van Ruysdael: *A River Scene with Cattle,* 1664.

Constable

J. R. Cozens: *Florence from near the Cascine*, ca. 1776-79.

Thomas Gainsborough: *The Fallen Tree*, mid-1750s. Minneapolis Institute of Arts.

John Crome: *The Beaters*, 1810. Viscountess of Halifax Collection.

Natural effect and technical bravura: Turner's *A Frosty Morning, Sunrise*, 1813. Tate Gallery, London.

Awkward earthiness: Constable's *The Leaping Horse*, 1825, 53 1/2 inches high. Royal Academy, London.

Constable

Bound by natural color, Constable intensified the "nature" look to make it the formal structure of his work: *The Lock*, 1824.

Cézanne had the principles of Impressionism to describe a new formal order: *The Small Bridge*, National Gallery, Washington.

An incisive and dramatic sepia wash drawing of a favorite scene: Constable's *View on the Stour, Dedham Church in the Distance*, after 1830, about actual size. Victoria & Albert Museum.

Constable

A Constable oil sketch of the view at *Dedham Mill,* ca. 1810-15 (?). Victoria & Albert Museum.

Constable's panoramic study of *Dedham Vale Seen from a Wooded Hill,* 19 1/4 inches high.

Constable was interested in sky changes in relation to the illumination of landscape and also as a subject in itself, recording wind direction and time of day on his sketches. His *Cirrus Clouds,* ca. 1822, is reproduced about actual size.

Weymouth Bay, 1816, 8 inches high (Victoria & Albert Museum) was sketched by Constable on his honeymoon trip to Dorset. The sky and its dramatic lighting of the bay dominate the scene.

covered an incredible amount of ground: the splendor of natural effect, technical bravura and, in *A Frosty Morning,* the kind of sentiment that so concerned Constable. He had also painted directly from nature with a fresh immediacy and inspired accuracy that for others must have not seemed worth the redoing. Where then did Constable fit in, laboriously following with his groping studies from nature? When he finally broke through it was in the realization that his concept of nature wasn't Romantic, that the energy he needed was not generated by Romantic concepts, but by a narrower, more concentrated vision, which, if not precisely realist, was more akin to Clare than to Wordsworth. The Romantic subject means that its mood governs its interpreter—it is the "sublime imperative" thrown back to the artist from his imagination. What Constable discovered was that the restricted view, the ordinary and the familiar, gave him time to think, to see, its very familiarity releasing his own subjective feelings. He could make the necessary mistakes, start

Constable's *Weymouth Bay,* ca. 1820, 20 3/4 inches high (National Gallery, London) is one of his elaborations of the subject and Constable himself considered it only a sketch. The massively modeled clouds give the sky an active role in the picture.

Constable's *On the Stour,* after 1830, approaches the spontaneity of an Impressionist surface (24 inches high); Phillips Collection.

Waterloo Bridge, ca. 1824, is on the "neat" side of Constable's two-sided manner (21 11/16 inches high); Cincinnati Museum.

Constable's *The Cenotaph,* 1836, depicts a memorial erected to Joshua Reynolds (52 inches high); National Gallery, London.

another version and ponder over notes. He was able to turn away from the subject and, in his studio, be "happy in front of a six-footer"; where inspiration is not in the moment but spread over a patient sequence of actions, he brooded on the meaning painting can have.

Because of this, the problem of Constable's two-sided manner, his "looseness" or "neatness," is not really a problem of contradiction. At times he was compelled to worry and fuss the paint, confused by hesitations and failure of energy. However the two versions of the *Leaping Horse* are not by different painters with contradictory aims, and the oil sketches are not the expression of the uninhibited "real" artist. His feeling for paint and his handling of it were not miraculous like Turner's. His training was long and arduous with side glances at many of his contemporaries. When he achieved confidence he used paint more expressively than anyone since Rembrandt. Turner and sometimes Constable, in his small sketches, used paint calligraphically and at the same time as the unifying skin over form, light and movement. It is aqueous, reflecting light from the first application. But Constable molds it, incises it like a sculptor, conscious of its weight and matching it to weight. His painting therefore asks to be looked closely into and at the same time sensed as structure and mass. Arriving at the small Constable gallery at the Tate, after rooms full of Turner, you feel almost physical discomfort, like bumping into the edges of heavy furniture. It was of course this awkward earthiness, not the trivial naturalism, that made Ruskin shudder. You have to look hard at these strange paintings, following their growth deep to the spreading and tenacious roots. While Cézanne had the principles of Impressionism to describe his new formal order, Constable was bound to naturalistic color. It is true he gave it superior force by breaking certain areas into complementaries, a device already practiced by many English painters. What he sought was to intensify the "nature" look, to make this look the formal structure of his painting, and, like Rembrandt, to match form to reality in its most naturalistic sense.

Did he tend to be sanctimonious? Perhaps nature worshippers are tinged with this. They parade a Quaker-like exclusiveness, a holier-than-thou superiority. Nature is a special revelation, a fount of goodness from whose holy waters only the morally superior may drink. Simplicity and purity are the prerogatives of certain places and persons and strictly reserved. "Think of the lovely valleys and the peaceful farmhouses of Suffolk forming a scene of exhibition to amuse the gay and frivolous Parisians." But if Constable was insular in his views of place or subject he certainly was not about the art of painting. He wished to situate this firmly within the body of what he considered to be the greatest art. His slightly provincial and evangelical musings on the poetry and goodness of rusticity were tempered by tough thinking about painting. He sets himself against the "ideal," the "divine," the "inspired," saying: "In such an age as this painting should be understood, not looked on with blind wonder, nor considered only as poetic aspiration, but as a pursuit, *legitimate, scientific* and mechanical"; and "We see nothing till we truly understand it." There is evidence in Constable's own

View of the Stour near Dedham, 1822, has Constable's usual steady light of midday in summer (51 inches high); Huntington Gallery, San Marino, Cal.

Constable's many views of Salisbury Cathedral are his most famous series. *Salisbury Cathedral from the River,*
ca. 1829, shows the maturing of a superbly live manner of direct working from nature, prophetic of Impressionism.

An earlier treatment, with massive loosely painted trees framing the tightly drawn cathedral:
The Cathedral from the Bishop's Garden, 1826, 35 inches high (Frick Coll.). Details right.

work of a struggle between the cool control and organization of objective fact and the moralizing poet-philosopher. In his best work the struggle is resolved, the understanding *is* the poetry and the charge which he made in later life against himself, "I have too often sacrificed the Beautiful to the Picturesque," no longer true.

His sketches of course are beautiful, particularly to modern taste: clean, limpid, with a certainty of rendering in color and execution. Painted out of doors between 1810 and 1830, they are a majestic harvest of the long years spent drawing in notebooks, copying and studying techniques in every painting he could lay his eyes on. This style of sketching was not really an innovation of Constable's. The desire to catch an evanescent effect of light and color is evident in English painting from the beginning of the century. But Constable introduces a directness, a sharper focusing of observed fact. He makes greater use of opaque paint. There is a sensation of speed, the paint is stabbed or stroked where changes of color or light are noted. The shorthand he used described the quick compression of noted facts dominated by the drama of cloud and light in the sky. There is an "expression" of space, not passive impressionism. It rebounds with the sharp force of a tennis ball hurled against a wall. The impact is physical, the concentrated energy of an assault on a narrow front. Where, in a Turner watercolor, the subject filters down through sensation purified by elimination, in Constable it is as if the accumulation of images (even if only implied or situated) is ordered into one overwhelming fact. He may have felt that a large stage was unsuited to the performance of this almost gymnastic act, that in his studio in front of a six-foot canvas this kind of immediacy of sensation would inevitably lead to stylistic emptiness. Three feet of green is different from one square inch. Furthermore there was the question of creating space, for every object in a Constable (even the sentiment) is subordinate to this. To make it more real, more surrounding, more enfolding, he would at times, it must be admitted, stifle his subject. This ennobling of space is pervasive in all his greatest work, and objects take their place in it like obedient children in the perfect family.

How far he influenced the 19th century is not very important in judging his stature as an artist. He is simply one of its greatest painters. He wanted to make great painting out of landscape. This was more important to him than devising new ways of doing it. The Victoria & Albert Museum is a good place to study Constable, not only because of the imposing amount of work in every medium, but adjoining there is an effective bird's-eye view of contemporary and later British painting. You can see the kind of world he was working in and what immediately followed. The Ionides Collection has examples of Delacroix, Courbet, Corot while further on there is a mixed lot of old masters illustrating just the sort of thing Constable most detested. Returning to the *Leaping Horse* and the sketches is a revelation. It is a shock of sudden understanding. A different dimension is given the rooms, the paintings thrust outwards with powerful insistence. Writing to Fisher he says: "It is the business of a painter not to contend with nature and put this scene (a valley filled with imagery 50 miles long) on a canvas of a few inches, but to make something out of nothing, in attempting which he must almost out of necessity become poetical." To define "poetical," to use it as leverage for the act of painting, was the challenge and final justification for his art. Whereas Linnell, Callcott and, in France, Rousseau were concerned with a poetic conception of nature, it was only an aura, an illustrative sentiment, persuasive at times as nostalgia evoking a lost paradise. For Constable these feelings were also part of his imagination, but he was obstinately, first and foremost, a painter. Over and over again he stresses the objective, scientific basis of painting. After his death it was difficult to see this and for a long time he was to remain the dim apostle of rural virtues. Art was at the beginning of a period of ideological polemic. To the Impressionists his murky naturalism was not what their own painting was about. Turner, yes; for with him color harmonies were carried to some extreme point and created a parallel to nature.

The case for Constable rests not on his role as a revolutionary—his direct influence was surely marginal—but on his success in creating a synthesis out of material which, psychologically and artistically, had much inherent contradiction and stress. He was one of the first de-professionalizers of art, in spite of desperate work to make himself a professional out of amateur material; he defined painting to mean an activity subject to choice, in its innocent inclinations closer to inspired amateurism. Rather than the new art, he symbolizes the new artist who, standing alone, armed only with the antennas of feeling and character, senses his way to self-discovery.

By Elizabeth C. Baker

Hans Hofmann

Abstract-Expressionism and color in New York, 1945-65

Elizabeth C. Baker is Managing Editor of ARTnews; her book on Roy Lichtenstein is due shortly from Penguin.

Hans Hofmann

Until very recently, Hofmann has been somewhat *hors concours* in that perpetual re-shuffling of hierarchies and reputations which is inevitable as the present tries to come to terms with the recent past. This is not entirely surprising. From many points of view, he is one of the most complicated and difficult of major American artists; his work is nowhere close to being fully understood. He was a crucial catalyst during Abstract-Expressionism's formative years, timely and extremely influential as a teacher. Yet as his painting matured, he was more and more out of step with immediate history in terms of his own work.

A figure of formidable prestige during much of his long lifetime, Hofmann was warmly praised and perceptively analyzed by the generation of historians and critics who grew up with Abstract-Expressionism. Yet there has been a hiatus of serious attention since a few years before his death in 1966, and he has not been given a major exhibition[1] since the one at the Museum of Modern Art in 1963. Perhaps his fame, together with the intricately constituted monolith of a very large and infrequently-seen oeuvre have managed, for the better part of a decade, to preclude any close or continuous confrontation with his paintings.

However Hofmann is now the subject of lively interest on the part of many younger artists and critics. Part of the reason is very simply the result of a current painterly resurgence. He was, among leading figures of the painterly 1950s, one of the most painterly in a full-range way. Even so, the present return to paint, and Hofmann's significance in terms of his painterliness, are part of a larger situation which includes an attempt to recapture complexity for today's new art, and to find some room for the personality of the artist. In fact, a broad shift in perception appears to be taking place.

The most conspicuous and advanced art of the 1960s was engaged in a highly specialized, often abstruse refining, defining and innovating process. The other side of the brilliance and intellectual clarity of the best work of this period was a conscious narrowing of focus and sometimes a tendency to parsimoniousness. The past year or two have seen a decided contrast. It is now possible to make out certain links between a broad range of new modes, inclined to be comparatively inclusive, even permissive, and attitudes current in the 1950s. This clearly includes (although it does not end with) a diverse group of young painterly abstractionists.[2] For many of today's artists, Hofmann is a rich source of a profoundly complex, broader-than-formalist kind of painting which nevertheless encompasses much of the best of a formalist approach.[3]

Hofmann's career was characterized by diverse, wide-ranging investigations propelled by tremendous energy. These took place in what seemed to be all directions at once. The results for a long time appeared quite equivocal.

His work contradicted many of the cast-iron assumptions of the 1960s, and was problematical for the '50s as well. Reaching his peak in the early '60s heyday of impersonal, objective and progress-oriented styles, Hofmann seemed unorthodox, vacillating, chaotic, too emotional and romantic—after having seemed unorthodox, vacillating, chaotic, too eclectic and perhaps too premeditated a decade before. Prior to that his situation was even more complicated, in a way provisional, caught up with the emergence of America's first real avant-garde, its cultural milieu from the 1930s on, and its relation to European modernism.

The notion that Abstract-Expressionism had to be decisively "post-European" was often formulated in drastic terms, and the need to find new, non-European ways existed with a vengeance. Hofmann's large stylistic debt to Europe[4] seemed to fly in the face of all that. In addition, well into the 1950s Hofmann could work in numerous manners so apparently unrelated that he sometimes seemed to be operating in disguise.

Unlike other leading Abstract-Expressionists, Hofmann did not concentrate on establishing and working within a highly differentiated and immediately identifiable personal style. One does not feel, either, that his main objective was to produce masterworks—for a long time he was not bent on ultimate finalities. (He was often quoted as saying that if he found a single style to adhere to, he would no longer paint.)

Furthermore, his work did not appear to be, nor seem to aspire to be "new." In fact, Hofmann was not an innovator in the sense which came to be considered pretty much *de rigueur* for important 20th century art. He is exceptional, nearly (although one could discuss Gorky and to a certain extent de Kooning in this respect) among the leaders of the New York School for his lack

Left: Detail of Hans Hofmann's *Joy Sparks of the Gods, 3,* 1965, 84 inches high. Courtesy Emmerich Gallery.

Untitled watercolor, 1936, 9 3/4 inches high.

of straining after originality. He did, of course, invent; however his inventions tended to remain subsidiary or episodic. For example, his famous early (pre-Pollock) use of poured or dripped paint skeins as a major compositional element was not purposefully explored by him, nor were other of his stylistic particularities. It is true that drip and splash techniques play an important, often flashy role in certain later works, but he employs them sporadically as familiar elements from a much broader vocabulary. Hofmann represents something of a special case in recent avant-garde art; he stands at the crux of the unsolved problem of defining the relationship between innovation and quality.

There is not doubt that the large space Hofmann occupied in the minds of several generations of his "contemporaries" (all so much younger than he) had overwhelmingly to do with his powerful influence as a teacher and personality; even his "old-master" status (reviews of exhibitions for more than 20 years keep referring to him as "venerable") worked to the detriment of his reputation as a painter. His famous pedagogy may have suggested an academicism in his own art; indeed, there are some paintings where

"problem solving" of a didactic nature is strongly felt. But the balance has shifted with the passing of time and today, Hofmann is not really thought of as a teacher—in fact, it is no longer even possible for those who did not know him to recreate his enormous significance in that realm. Today there is no ambivalence in choosing between the influential, forcefully elaborated theory and the paintings. Whatever the hesitations, cross-currents, complex sources and interim irresolutions of Hofmann's course, he *did* finally emerge as an unequivocally major painter; this outweighs all of his other activities—and at the same time revalidates them.

Recently, there have been signs of a slackening of pressure both in the direction of newness, and towards the formally compressed, single statement. Hofmann's work now stands in a peculiar and interesting relationship to that touchy and preconception-ridden "ideal" of innovation, which has suddenly begun to loom as a threatening short-circuit to an artist's full development. Hofmann never short circuited himself on this (or any other) account. Instead, his diversity and breadth, his multi-layered intentions, his shifting, protean imagination, his knowledgeable incorporation of tradition, all now look vital and appealing. It appears more and more that it was a source of strength that he was able to embody many aspects of the modern tradition at once, with no real sense of contradiction, without giving himself up to any one of them. It turns out, too, that the early "less good" works have their own distinct, if perhaps less accessible virtues. The sense of confusion he can project is in many ways superficial, and has certainly been exaggerated by recent orthodox taste. This "problematic" aspect could just as well be thought of as openness, capacity for change, or operating within an unusually broad and unspecific consistency. His propensity to combine, recombine, shift, make new by altering of context— all his permutations of a strongly felt relational approach ("Relation is the product of a hypersensitive creative mind," Hofmann said) make an art with a particular truth to it which is once again challenging in its difficulties.

Hofmann's cosmopolitanism, and the perhaps excessive possibilities which it offered him, may be the key to his slowness of development— as well as to the stunning authority of his late works. In comparison to many of his American colleagues, Hofmann did not seem particularly avant-garde; yet all his life he had been part of an avant-garde which was an accepted European reality. Among the artists connected with the embryonic New York scene, only John Graham and to an extent Gorky and de Kooning shared Hofmann's quality of cosmopolitanism. They too, of course, were European born. While Hofmann, once permanently established in New York, could be considered as American as de Kooning or Gorky, a significant difference existed in his having been an adult participant (albeit a fringe one) in the pre-World-War I Paris avant-garde.

It is interesting to compare the results of his situation to the careers of such American innovators as, for example, Pollock or Kline. It has been pointed out[5] that in the 1940s avant-gardism came with the impact of a tremendous personal revelation to some of these men—almost, indeed, as a religious conversion. This conversion was transmuted into an art of great innovative intensity, stressful risk, brilliance and, as it turned out, extreme precariousness. For some of these artists their most innovative periods were relatively short-lived. Little room for maneuvering seemed left to them after their individual vision had been worked through. By contrast, Hofmann paid a price gradually, over the long period of time when he appeared to be floundering in unassimilated diversity. But thanks to his rock-like staying power, not to mention his imaginative efforts of no less intensity than those of his more innovative colleagues, his cosmopolitan past was finally brought into brilliant fusion with his increasingly individual, forward-looking art.

The timing of Hofmann's development (which, it must be remembered, reached its high point as the artist approached his 80s), is fascinating, slightly preposterous and bizarre. There is something very special about those rare individuals who produce extraordinary work in a late burst of productive and inventive energy. Hofmann worked right up to his death in 1966 at 85; quantities of his finest paintings date from his last few years. (Titian probably died in his early 90s, and the radical nature of his very last works is well known; one thinks also of Monet, who died at 86; Michelangelo, at 89; Matisse, at 85; Degas, at 83; Bonnard, at a relatively young 80—all of whom did major work late in life.) But Hofmann is almost unique in his precise circumstances: most other artists of late achievement were outstanding figures in their youth. Hofmann, whether done out of his early phases by circumstances (war, teaching, too much avant-garde art) or simply developing at an unusually slow pace, had an entire career which was comparatively late. His full-time reengagement with painting in the late 1930s began when he was in his late 50s. His most consistent and personal work started to emerge 20 years after that.

In his youth, Hofmann was evidently somewhat eclipsed by a period of overpowering invention, a not incomprehensible circumstance for a young artist who frequented the circles around Matisse, Braque, Picasso, Delaunay et al. in pre-1914 Paris.[6] Forced by war to remain in Munich from 1915 on (where his studio was filled with stored Kandinskys for the duration), his long teaching phase began, and a protracted interim during which he painted practically not at all.[7] Fame of his Munich school spread during the '20s; conditions in Europe and an invitation to teach for a summer in California resulted in a permanent move to the U.S. in the early '30s, and establishment of his school in New York.

Teaching must have had something to do with keeping his own work on ice. Perhaps his devoted propagation in Munich and then in New York of French avant-gardism impelled him to a kind of passivity during what would normally have been his most competitive

Hans Hofmann

and highly motivated years. In any case, it was only after closing his school in 1958, at age 78 with over 40 years of teaching behind him, that he turned all his energies to his own painting. In the years left, he was able to draw on newly released energies from within and without, as the 1960s began.

The accident of a very long career seems sometimes to confer prerogatives of operating substantially outside history, and of making choices more daring than those available to the more historically-bound, worldly and career-conscious young. Becoming a-historical late in life allowed Hofmann to bring about unexpected and ultimately highly original transformations in his work.

Hofmann's work does not unfold in a meaningful chronology, or at least not one which can be abbreviated here in any useful way. However when one considers his work, a number of generalities come to mind.

It is clear that, despite the look of many *individual* works of being spontaneous almost to the point of caprice, all thoughts of romantic frenzy or pure unmediated fancy or emotion must be removed when one takes into account Hofmann's manipulation of paint. One is not accustomed to think of systematization of pictorial elements occurring in a style that is not geometric and fully pre-planned; yet in Hofmann there are distinct categories of paint-application which produce distinctly separate and separable types of form. This is not to say that Hofmann resorts to a systematic usage of them, but these comprise a clearly recognizable syntax which constantly crops up in the most variable expressive contexts. His work is, in a way, a kind of laboratory of the painterly—an exploration of painterly range, a

Exuberance, 1955, 50 inches high. Albright-Knox Gallery, Buffalo.

The Garden, 1956, 60 inches high. Univ. Art Museum, Berkeley.

Birdcage – Variation 2, 1956-58, 60 inches high.
Collection Mr. and Mrs. Saul Z. Cohen, Larchmont, N.Y.

catalogue of what paint can attain and a loose codifying of its attributes. What his paintings say visually is not entirely in line with the rhetorical romanticism of his titles, nor with the paintings' often grandiose emotional implications. For his painterliness develops into an almost linguistic equivalent, in the perspective of his whole oeuvre. A painting like *Joy Sparks of the Gods, 3* (see page 106) is typical of certain very large works produced after the entire vocabulary was fully evolved, and takes delight in running through the incredible technical virtuosity he commanded.

This "exhaustive" attitude to the manipulation of paint takes him into what often seems a purely physical reliance on specific materiality, in his middle (1950s) period especially. Many of his early '50s paintings invite comparison to the *matière* of late School of Paris paintings. There are certain traits Hofmann shares, on occasion, with such French artists as Mathieu (decorative calligraphic accents of wet-squeezed tube pigment);

Fautrier (troweled and slathered swaths); Riopelle (trickily laid-on multicolor knife-tip strokes); de Staël (fudge-textured blocky abutments with a vaguely landscape look); Soulages (big sweeps of a wide brush indicating structural slabs). It is reasonable to surmise that Hofmann was aware of the European school as it was in the late '40s (he visited Paris and showed there in 1949). He once said, "I can do anything as long as it is esthetically justified." Indeed, his essays in this direction generally absorb such reminiscent mannerisms in a bravura performance notable for its vehemence, characteristic blazing color and his refusal to fix on any single manner. The Hofmann of the early 1950s may be what the late School of Paris should have produced but didn't.

Among the Abstract-Expressionists, Hofmann and de Kooning were the two main painterly colorists. De Kooning is a superb, intuitive and highly original

Magnum Opus, 1962, 84 inches high. University Art Museum, Berkeley.

Bedeutungsvolles Ahnen, 1965, 60 inches high. Private Coll.

The Scorpion, 1962, 84 inches high.
Emmerich Gallery, New York.

Little Cherry (Renate Series No. 1), 1965,
84 inches high. Estate of Hans Hofmann.

colorist; his color is inextricably part of a dense, quasi-figurative, largely linear style. Hofmann's use of color is quantitative, more overtly spatial, and directly related to the textural properties of paint.

Some clue to this intentional physicality can be gained from Hofmann's description of color as ground-up rubies, sapphires, emeralds and topazes. This corroborates the impression that his habitual colors are prismatic, pure, very "natural." However this kind of color gives way to a more exotic and artificial gamut in many of his '60s works. For example, in *Capriccio* (1962) he combines a strange, thin, smoky terra-cotta wash with a stinging magenta rectangle, and he puts acid green and yellow inside that. (The values are, typically, so close that in black and white photographs, they nearly merge.) This coincides with the precious and bizarre color tastes increasingly to be favored by many younger artists during the 1960s.

Hofmann associates color with light. His own words are precise in this regard: "In nature, light creates the color; in the picture, color creates, light. Every color shade emanates a very characteristic light... The luminous quality of a work depends not only upon the light-emanating quality of every color, but predominantly upon the relation of these particular qualities..." The inclusion of a great deal of white, either painted (as in *Birdcage, Variation 2*) or the white canvas ground (*Capriccio, Magnum Opus, Joy Sparks of the Gods*) is often crucial to his effects of extreme luminosity.

Hofmann had a protracted involvement with the figure. This was directly connected to his keeping European

modernism alive. Picasso and Matisse both are very much present in these works.

This phase seems to have taken him from the '20s into the '40s. During the time when he did not paint, he evidently drew incessantly. There are portfolios from these years containing thousands of drawings and watercolors.[8]

Some of his work from the late '30s was very free and experimental with little in the way of "academic modernist" content (see, for instance, the untitled watercolor on page 109). However, much of what he produced in the middle '40s (along with the contemporary production of Pollock, Gottlieb, et al.) seems to emphasize how far the available repertory of semi-abstraction as it then stood has been run through, and the difficulty of extending its range; powerful as much of this work is, it partakes of that "making modern art" awkwardness which seems to be synonymous with that '40s period look.

Related to this is Hofmann's skilful, often aggravating imposition of Synthetic-Cubist linear skeletons in a number of figural works which, though painted, are essentially draftsmanship with a little color. (It is odd how much some of these seem to prefigure the quasi-anthropomorphic planar geometries in the sculpture of David Smith.)

Automatic techniques were important to Hofmann from the 1930s on. Automatism must be distinguished from Surrealism as a whole, but its Surrealist origins must be recognized. Hofmann's automatically-derived linear passages were a source of suggestive, mythological or

Flaming Lava, 1965, 72 inches high. Private Collection.

Hans Hofmann

natural subject matter in the 1940s and '50s, as such titles as *The Birth of Taurus, The Lark, The Prey, Bald Eagle* attest. This descriptive interpretation of fortuitously suggestive shapes is different from the subconscious-probing subject matter which the Surrealists extracted from automatism, but the connection is there. Hofmann once said that for him the major innovators were Kandinsky, Mondrian, Arp and Miro. While the last two would seem to have the most bearing on automatism and exploited accident, it is useful to consider Hofmann's improvisational line in relation to Kandinsky's as well. Another incidental link with the Surreal (i.e., Matta) are some Hofmann's organic-mechanistic concoctions, as in *Delight.*

Hofmann's automatism seems to have more to do with speed and intuition and accident than with the search for subconscious direction of a genuinely Surrealistic (and thus extra-visual) nature. He is interested in perfecting the instant flying touch.

Spontaneity and accident are as inherently controllable as any other technique. Even Hofmann's "accidents" are induced, or, more specifically, the degree of accidentality to be induced is semi-predictable.

Automatism usually implies line—a painterly style of drawing is extremely conducive to its incorporation. It also lends itself to free deployment of pigment in areas. Hofmann used it both ways. At one time or another he ran the gamut of automatist usages: calligraphy, primitivistic signs, biomorphisms, plant-type configurations, elusive figural suggestions, space-producing capacities, atmospheric washes, suggestions of voids and vastnesses, drastic changes of scale.

These usages in Hofmann are a constant in the midst of flux. They start to appear in the late '30s—*Red Trickle* (1939) is a poured-paint tangle of liquid red line superimposed on a spidery stiff-looking linear understructure applied by brush. *Fantasia* (1943) has no armature whatever under the freely poured and dripped paint. These paintings, of course, antedate Pollock's drip works[9] (although they do not antedate Wols). A virtuosic extension of similar techniques re-emerges in the late '50s and is a major and spectacular element in the more spontaneous of his 1960s works. Altogether, it is clear that automatism was as frutiful for Hofmann as it was for Pollock or Gorky.

Solid rectangles of color started tentatively to emerge from Hofmann's lush impastos in the middle 1950s, and were decisively established by the late '50s. It is not entirely clear, from looking at the work of the '50s, how these were arrived at. They can be seen as evolving from his mosaic-touch paintings of the middle '50s.[10] They can also be seen as resulting from a solidifying and isolating of Synthetic-Cubist planes (visible as semi-isolated elements in such still-lifes as *Magenta and Blue*). They might also be considered in terms of Picasso's and especially Braque's Analytical Cubist paint usages—generally considered a rigidly conceptual and intellectual style, Analytical Cubism (and especially Braque's) could be excruciatingly sensitive in its execution. In this respect Hofmann's rectangles might be considered an expansion of Cubist paint touches, squared, taking the faceting strokes of 1911 into the mosaic surface of the '50s and then into larger painterly slabs, and finally the rectangles clearly stated.

This might seem to overlook the obvious precedent of Mondrian, Neo-Plasticism, Suprematist squares, all of '20s and '30s geometric abstraction, as well as such contemporaries of Hofmann as Diller or Bolotowsky, but in fact the final form, obviously indebted to Mondrian, which the rectangles assumed was a long time in emerging from an apparently unschematic series of stages.

The compositions of solid rectangles are very different from those isolated rectangles which float in front of or in the midst of much loose paint. Some of the titles refer to architecture: *Cathedral, Combinable Wall, Golden Wall*, etc. The rectangles in these works can be read as blocks each with its own weight. Yet sometimes the gravity and logic of these "solids" is metamorphosed into atmosphere. Architectonic passages are quite likely to be contradicted in this way in adjacent sections of the same work.

The rectangles are a beneficially arbitrary format in which to manipulate color. They pretty much dispose of residual landscape hints. The size of the rectangles in relation to each other and in relation to the picture as a whole make an extremely flexible system for indicating space. When similarly proportioned and linked in chromatic sequences, they make an efficient, obvious, and already much elucidated depth device. Much has been made of the relationship to the picture surface and to the framing edge; yet it seems redundant to call attention to their frontality; indeed, Hofmann seems to make something of their independence of the edge, instead occasionally tipping them, cropping them, signaling their manipulatability in depth, their existence in a fluid medium, all within the vestiges of a conventional, center-weighted space.

Hofmann bows to no geometric rigidity. He uses geometry as freely as his other elements. Energy infuses his slabs as much if not more than his gestures. His gestural passages can be lyrical or serene next to the aggression of these ostensibly "passive" solids.

Hofmann's work of the 1960s has not all been exhibited yet. A detailed consideration of this impressive culminating phase will have to await a comprehensive showing.

The late paintings sum up his tendency to exhaust the capacities of the medium—which is an exceedingly flexible one. In them there are thrown paint, chunky swirls, spattered mists, transparent bleeds and washes, squeezed calligraphy opposed by the rectangles, which take the brushwork into a stringent realm. Often in the late works when he picks up a brush, it is to execute a disciplined, hard rectangle. The other paint-effects are often not made with the brush.

Generally speaking, open, partially covered surfaces increase. In such paintings as *The Scorpion* or *Otium cum Dignitate,* there is a delicate and masterly first-shot (unrepainted) deployment of tiny rectangles and large free areas, fusing the complexity of a fully-worked out painting with the openness and luminosity of the voids. Virtuoso pieces like this exist concurrently with more lushly saturated items like *Summer Over the Land* (with landscape references still) and the more weighty large-rectangle compositions, which in his last year press close to the picture surface in a gravely monumental expansion of fewer units.

It is clear that in his last phases Hofmann was painting in terms which were newly opened up by the various changing currents of '60s color-field painting. His relationship with the stain painters of the '60s has yet to be unraveled in terms of specifics; it is clear enough, however, in the work, that he was involved in a fruitful interchange with this group. (In some works, such as *Magnum Opus, Memoria in Aeternum, Silent Reverence,* pure-hued rectangles are foils to the intimidating obscurity of almost monochrome, brownish, color-suffused clouds; these have a certain resemblance to some of Morris Louis' more turgid and opaque monochrome

Veils.) His spaces become shallower and expansive. His openness, artificial colors, transparent, mat and thinned-down surfaces, large plane areas, unitary forms and hard edges all give evidence of his compatibility with the work of much younger artists. Indeed, his conduciveness to stimulation by such ideas indicates that they were at least as compatible as painterly expressionism with his original predilections to both clarity and theory.

1. There has been no comprehensive retrospective of Hofmann's work. The 1963 Museum of Modern Art exhibition (organized before his last few and very fruitful years) was never intended to be comprehensive. The only place to see a large group of Hofmanns is Berkeley's University Art Museum, to which the artist gave 47 major works from all periods; they are continually on exhibition there.
2. Also, might the current spate of "body art" (a loose category for those artists who document, photograph, cast from, measure with, even lacerate their own flesh) be seen as an extreme extension of the autobiographical content of Abstract Expressionism, via Happenings?
3. Hofmann's art theory was an important influence on formalist criticism of recent years. Clement Greenberg explicitly mentions in "New York Painting only Yesterday" (ARTnews, Summer, 1957; republished as "The Late Thirties in New York" in *Art and Culture,* Beacon Press, 1961) that a series of public lectures given by Hofmann in 1938-39 "were crucial" for him.
4. Fauvism, especially Matisse, Cubism, especially Braque, Delaunay and a little later, Kandinsky, Mondrian, Klee, etc. Hofmann was in Paris from 1904 to 1914.
5. Elaine de Kooning, "Kline and Rothko," Art News Annual XXVII, 1957-58.
6. While the evidence is mostly lost, it appears both by Hofmann's own account and those who knew him that he produced little during these years. He worked from the figure at the Grande Chaumière school in 1904 (Matisse was doing likewise at the same time and place), became friends with Braque, good friends with Delaunay.
7. Fritz Bultman (ARTnews, Sept. 1963) mentions some Hofmann paintings from the '20s.
8. Ibid.
9. A number of writers have casually linked Hofmann with Pollock. It would be interesting to know more precisely the relationship between Hofmann's and Pollock's use of drip techniques. Both were associated with Peggy Guggenheim's Art of This Century Gallery; Hofmann student Lee Krasner married Pollock.
10. Hofmann did some actual mosaics in New York buildings but they seem unconnected to the unit-idea he was developing in paint.

By John Ashbery

Willem de Kooning

A suite of new lithographs translates his famous brushstroke into black and white

John Ashbery is Executive Editor of ARTnews and a poet; his
Three Poems will be published early in 1972 by Viking.

Willem de Kooning

In the fall of 1970 Willem de Kooning began a series of 20 black and white lithographs, his first work in this form except for two inconclusive stabs at it in 1960 and 1967 whose results apparently didn't satisfy him. The reasons for his taking up a medium seemingly so foreign to his temperament at the age of 66 are not entirely clear; or rather, one can point to some possible ones but they seem no more nor less relevant to the work itself than his immediate sources of inspiration generally are: they are curiously independent of it and as it were co-existing with it.

One impulse, nevertheless, for the series may have come as the result of a trip in 1969 to Japan which happened, like his other rare journeys out of this country since he arrived here from Holland in 1926, almost by chance, at the suggestion of his friend and dealer, Xavier Fourcade who was going there on business. Though he probably had never intended to visit Japan, once he got there de Kooning looked closely at Japanese art, particularly Sumi ink drawings. Some aspects of the lithographs that were to come later suggest a parody of the parody of nature that Sumi drawings, in a sense, already are.

Another might be the friendly insistence of Irving Hollander, who with his partner Fred Genis runs Hollanders Workshop on New York's Lower East Side. For years de Kooning had rejected similar proposals from graphics studios and, knowing him as an artist for whom the notion of "finishing" a work is somehow irrelevant, one can understand his refusal. For the lithography stone or plate has to be considered finished by somebody before the printing process can take place and the work come into existence, however tentatively it may wish to do so. And the idea of a series of prints being pulled menaces even further this tentativeness, this openness to further suggestion that is at the center of de Kooning's art. Furthermore the mystique of craftsmanship and the almost guild-like reverence for fine printing that prevail in the better studios are also alien to de Kooning's rugged spontaneity, although, having begun life as an artisan (sign-painting and window-display, founded on solid practical training at the Rotterdam Academy), he might have felt an obscure

Willem de Kooning: *Weekend at Mr. and Mrs. Krisher,* one of a series of lithographs done in 1970-71. This one exists in two formats; the smaller (42½ inches high) is reproduced here.

impulse to return briefly to the closed, comfortable certainties that the exercise of a manual skill can give. No doubt too the informal atmosphere of the two-man Hollanders Workshop (Fred Genis is also Dutch and speaks English with an accent almost like de Kooning's all-but-inimitable one) made the suggestion more attractive: the pieties of craft are totally alien to the workshop, whose casual ambience is more like that of a garage, though the level of craftsmanship is high.

Still another cause may be the restless desire for change and expansion that has always characterized de Kooning. After the "Women" of the '50s he moved into the "Landscape" and "Parkway" pictures which were simultaneously topography and woman looked at too closely to be legible as such. These in turn precipitated the "Women in the Country" paintings of the late '60s, in which the landscape seems to have given birth to its women before retreating once again to the sidelines, leaving behind only the barest reference to itself. The exuberant, often strident chromaticism and the luxuriant paint in these late, great pictures may have caused him to look for an antidote which the restrictions of the lithography process and the more or less mandatory black-on-white provided. (De Kooning had tried experimenting with color lithography but gave it up for the time being as too complicated; it requires that each color be drawn separately on a single plate or stone; these are then superimposed in the printing process. Having learned a great deal about technique while doing the black and white lithographs, he intends to try color lithography again.)

In a way, the lithographs have an oblique relation to the paintings that preceded them similar to that which his black and white paintings of the late '40s have to their predecessors. In the latter case, the tautly organized, hot-colored figure paintings of the middle '40s were gradually supplanted by paintings like *Attic* and *Mailbox.* Here, drained of color, the shapes turn abstract, welling up meanwhile and pushing toward the front of the canvas' shallow space to produce an almost claustrophobic feeling that somehow soothes after the sustained euphoria of, for example, the ca. 1944 *Woman* or of *Pink Angels.* Color and the human form have been purged and rendered ideal and remote; but in the process new pressures have built up which will in turn require puncturing when the time is ripe. In the same way, the vehement physicality of the "Women in the Country" leads to an equally vehement renunciation of

Willem de Kooning working on a lithograph at
Hollanders Workshop, New York.

physicality in the earlier lithographs such as *Love to Wakako* or *Weekend at Mr. and Mrs. Krisher.* Subsequently there is an almost nostalgic return to the look of the Women, followed by a later period in which this dualism disappears and the artist begins again coining new words with the alphabet he has just learned, and where references to landscape, body and undecipherable abstract notations combine, proliferate, disappear or collide, sometimes all at once, to explode finally in the four lithographs done after the series was completed. Here de Kooning at last took to drawing directly on the stone slab, a process that had somewhat intimidated him before. He had at first used transfer-paper which he liked because he could throw away the sheets or cut them up and combine them. He also drew on zinc plates, but there is something about the sheer monumentality of a lithography stone that makes the most impetuous artist think twice before attacking it directly. At any rate, in the four post-series lithographs, the surface of the stone erupts into a dazzling over-all field of activity, as though *Attic* had exploded in a joyful apotheosis into the night sky. The effect is something like a sudden orchestral *tutti* coming after solo passages.

The earlier lithographs with their Zen austerity and kineticism (*Love to Wakako* could be the visual equivalent of the Zen novice's getting hit over the head with a stick when he least expects it during meditation) are,

however, worlds apart from de Kooning's previous black and white pictures and, in several cases, from the main tendencies in his work as a whole. The Sumi "influence," if such it can be called, seems fairly apparent in the lithographs just mentioned and in a beautiful, somewhat denser one called *Reflections—to Kermit for Our Trip to Japan,* in which the "rivers and mountains without end" of a Japanese scroll are turned inside out to produce a perverse effect of calm. But these fairly explicit references do not intrude on the "meaning" of a particular picture—they remain contiguous to it, just as his early Ingres-like drawing of Elaine de Kooning isn't an homage to Ingres or an *exercice du style* but a completely original work occupying the manner of another artist in order to re-make it new. Allusions to other styles in de Kooning's work take place almost by chance, like a reference in a conversation that touches on a number of disparate topics without attempting to emphasize any one in particular. He is saying that anything that can be formulated in visual terms has a value for this reason and only for this reason—it is a part and a part only of the totality of the work which surrounds the viewer in a continuum where parts cease to matter.

Love to Wakako and *Weekend at Mr. and Mrs. Krisher* with their scudding stabs of painterly black line (set down so quickly that the spatters and bubbles in the ink are preserved like fossils) look like non-functional ver-

Willem de Kooning

Love to Wakako, 45 inches high.

Reflections—to Kermit for Our
Trip To Japan, 50½ inches high.

Landing Place,
28½ inches high.

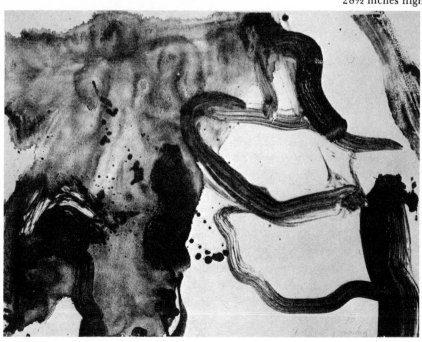

Willem de Kooning

Clam Digger, 40 inches high.

Valentine, 37 inches high.

Figure at Gerard Beach, 40 inches high.

Mother and Child, 28½ inches high.

Woman in Amagansett, 28½ inches high.

Woman with Corset and Long Hair, 37 inches high.

The Marshes, 40½ inches high.

Big, 40 inches high.

Beach Scene, 37 inches high.

Table and Chair, 29 3/4 inches high.

Japanese Village, 28 inches high.

Willem de Kooning

Sting Ray, 51 inches high.

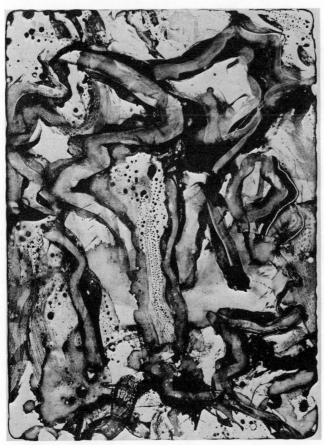

Landscape at Stanton Street, 29 3/4 inches high.

sions of the attempt to pick out salient points in a new space like the space in Kline's black and white paintings. We know by now that de Kooning doesn't feel impelled to joust with space, to make exploratory forays into it. It is all around him; he knows it "like his pocket" as the French say, and its seething jungle of forms is here merely invisible, offstage rather than absent. Nor does the allegorical "richness" of black on white (as in Kline or in Pollock's black paintings of the early 1950s) really interest him. Though he is at times throughout the series happy to conjugate the nuances of black—crisp or velvety, thin or gooey—with a virtuoso's relish, more often than not it is the poorness of black that he is calling attention to. Many of the blacks look almost grizzled, and sometimes all nuances are lost in murky passages where no attempt is made to distinguish one kind of black from another. Some of the lithographs are printed on a dull beige stock suggesting cheap wrapping paper or newsprint, further muffling any monochrome elegance and making them seem humble and awkward, two qualities he seems to like in the things he loves.

Weekend marks the first appearance in the series of the curious mushroom-like shape that suggests a little house, here floating on a band of black cloud perhaps; he takes it up later in the strange *Table and Chair,* an comparatively straightforward, Expressionistic rendering of some bits of organic furniture. This same shape reappears as an explicitly phallic mountain in *Japanese Village* (there is a 19th-century erotic Japanese print which similarly shows a mountain in the shape of a phallus, towering over a peaceful village). There is nothing to be said about this new shape, however nor about the peculiar mantis-like one at the bottom of *Weekend* which has become a swarm in *Wah Kee Spareribs.* They are merely examples of how de Kooning can, when he feels like it, invent what Wallace Stevens called "a completely new set of objects." There are other times when this doesn't interest him at all, and indeed one of his important unstated assumptions is that it is good not to do the same thing all the time, even at the risk of doing nothing: this too will eventually take its place in the scheme of things.

After this promising and novel beginning, de Kooning seems to be turning to thoughts of how the themes that have recently preoccupied him will fit the exigencies of the new medium. *Mother and Child, Woman in Amagansett, Figure at Gerard Beach* are lush, horizontal

126

Minnie Mouse, 30 inches high. Both this lithograph and *Landscape at Stanton Street* (opposite) were
done after the series of 20 was completed, and were drawn by de Kooning directly on the lithography stone.

variations on the theme of the landscape-woman; here, perhaps because he feels himself in familiar territory, de Kooning allows himself the leisure for elegance: the blacks of *Mother and Child* have that crisp, freshly-crayoned look that is so exhilarating in Bonnard's lithographs, for instance. Another figure, *Clam Digger,* is a revised version of an earlier lithograph; its elegance is the coarse elegance of a squat, bawdy Japanese figurine. (Clam diggers are common on eastern Long Island where de Kooning lives; the name is also used for a vodka, tomato and clam-juice cocktail served in the bar cars of the Long Island Rail Road. The *gaudeamus igitur* air of de Kooning's toiler of the sea suggests that the title might be an allusion to both).

In works such as *Beach Scene, Woman with Corset and Long Hair, Table and Chair, Japanese Village, Marshes* and *Big,* de Kooning gives the impression of advancing boldly into the medium and creating new forms uniquely suited and sometimes purposely inappropriate to it. *Marshes* and *Big* are two which he at first thought of publishing separately—according to Fred Genis he considered them "too good," a comment which, to one familiar with de Kooning's wit, need not be taken as an adverse judgment on the rest of the series. Perhaps he meant that they are too full, too "realized"; that their teeming richness is out of keeping with the skimming allusiveness of many of the others. Certainly they are remarkable, particularly *Marshes,* whose congested field of black strokes reads both like a "mad" Zen monk's version of an iris garden and like a Japanese ideogram where the meaning and its figuration seem to move along parallel tracks, illuminating each other but destined never to meet. *Figure* and *Beach Scene* suggest the epigrammatic, enigmatic simplicity of early paintings like the untitled one of 1934 in John Becker's collection, yet here loosened enough to allow free play to the oozing ink with its moist and erotic overtones of beaches; and the "villages" are the odd bonuses that arrive seemingly out of nowhere when an artist has fought his way into familiarity with a new medium. The rage for re-ordering reaches a paroxysm in *Sting Ray,* with its two halves apparently cut from separate sheets of tracing paper and juxtaposed. Both halves are clogged with swarming, blotted shapes from which issue smeared trajectories that are in turn absorbed back into them. The title suggests that the globular forms are swollen with venom, and the two halves could refer to a predator and its victim, but as usual there is no sense of tragedy, only an astrigent reality that isn't grim because it's real.

In what at this writing were his most recent lithographs, the four done directly on the stone, de Kooning has "gone after" the work with an energy and euphoria unusual even for him. It is as though the tense shorthand comments of a work like *Weekend* on the one hand and, on the other, the almost virulent, bulging masses of *Sting Ray* had erupted simultaneously, showering the surface of the picture with multiple allusions and proliferating forms. *The Preacher* is an outward-fanning field of repeated, interlocking gestures that suggests Boccioni (whom de Kooning admires while dismissing the concept of "Futurism" and of schools in general). The all-over *horror vacui* is unusual in de Kooning's work, for it is kinetic and fleeing rather than an unstable emulsion like the highly charged juxtapositions of works like *Attic. Landscape at Stanton Street* is kinetic, but here the strata seem to be collapsing inward into what Andrew Forge, writing on de Kooning, has called "reconcilable extremes of fragmentation and wholeness, violence and repose." A third recasts these galactic phenomena into a recognizable human shape—that of *Minnie Mouse,* if we are to believe de Kooning's joking title, and sure enough, there are the oversize pumps, the hair ribbon, the ferocious *moue.* But these are, again, a metaphor for Woman, for woman as watershed, collecting evasive feelings and anomalies of execution under a single heading and thus letting them live.

This is where things stand at the moment. The lithograph series as a whole seems to be opposing not only the austerity of monochrome but also a kind of discipline which still has room for moments of storytelling and sensuality, to the ecstatic, ecdysiastic world of "Women in the Country," a sort of Eden situated, like Dante's, on top of the mountain of purgatory. That there is no foretelling the future as far as de Kooning's work is concerned is of course obvious. All that we know is that it will change, and in art, in a sense, any change has to be for the better, since it shows that the artist hasn't yet given in to the ever-present temptation to stand still and that his constantly menaced vitality is emitting signals.

By Carter Ratcliff

Painterly vs. Painted

The new "painterly" abstraction is found lost in the painted

Carter Ratcliff contributes frequently to art
magazines here and abroad. He is also a poet and a
publisher of little magazines such as *Seaplane* and *Cicada*.

Painterly vs. Painted

From the late '30s until 1947, Jackson Pollock's paintings grew more "painterly"; that is, his brushwork became heavier, more energetic, messier. But painterliness has received a precise formal definition from Heinrich Wölfflin: it is a "surrender to mere visible appearance"; it merges objects, reducing "the appearance of the world [to] a shifting semblance." Painterliness takes on its full definition in opposition to linearity: the painterly is "the depreciation of line."[1] The painterly and the linear define a range of formal possibilities whose limits they give with their symmetrical opposition.

Wölfflin expands the opposition *painterly/linear* to *recession/plane, open/closed, unity/multiplicity* and *clear/unclear.*[2] These "five pairs of concepts...involve each other...we could call them five different views of the same things."[3] The expanded versions of the *painterly/linear* opposition apply well enough to Pollock's early work. A way of establishing his painterliness is to point out that it makes his images unclear (in comparison, say, with the images in the paintings he made in 1934-35 under the influence of Thomas Hart Benton); that his canvases are unified rather than built up from a harmony of clearly delineated elements; that these unified compositions are better characterized as open than as closed. The *recession/plane* opposition doesn't apply very well here, but one can say that until 1947 Pollock worked within the tradition given its formal description by Wölfflin's "pairs of concepts." This is not to endorse the specific form of Wölfflin's descriptive apparatus; it is to suggest that, however much refinement it has required since it appeared, it is based on a correct intuition of the way possibilities have traditionally presented themselves to Western artists, from the early Renaissance through the modern period.

Pollock always spoke as if his entire career were enclosed by this range of possibilities. He said in an interview in 1950 that "modern art," which he took himself to be representing, is "part of a long tradition dating back with Cézanne, up through the Cubists, the post-Cubists, to the painting being done today."[4] By placing himself in this way, Pollock implicitly accepted Wölfflin's "pairs of concepts," but after 1947 they no longer applied to his work. Pollock rejected them, along

Heavy brushwork, but "painted rather than painterly": Robert Ryman, untitled, 1970, oil on fiberglass, about actual size.

with the tradition to which they refer. To understand the meaning of this rejection will require a closer look at Wölfflin's method.

Wölfflin attempts to be neutral in applying his descriptive apparatus: "it is not a difference of quality if the Baroque departed from the ideals of the age of Dürer and Raphael, but, as we said, a different attitude toward the world." However, in describing the transformation from one pole of an opposition to the other, he betrays himself. The painterly is a "depreciation" of the linear; in the development from plane to recession, the plane is "discounted"; the relatively open Baroque has its own form of closure, but Renaissance design "may be taken as *the* form of closed composition"; Renaissance multiplicity shows "harmony," Baroque unity follows from the "subordination" of discrete pictorial elements; the Renaissance "ideal of perfect clarity" was "voluntarily sacrificed" by the Baroque.[5] For Wölfflin the Renaissance is the ideal—it is good—and the Baroque is a falling away from the ideal—it is, in effect, bad. His oppositions can thus be expanded: *Renaissance=linear= good/bad=painterly=Baroque.*

Painterly/linear is a local derivation of *bad/good.* To follow this transformation one must obviously leave the realm of formal description. One leaves it in another way by noting that Wölfflin's last transformation of *painterly/linear,* that is, *unclear/clear,* recurs in rationalist philosophy. The distinction between what is conceptually clear and what is not is crucial to Descartes' attempt to establish "the ultimate classes of real things." In the course of his argument, *clear/unclear* is transformed into *true/untrue.*[6] Elsewhere, Descartes' version of the ontological argument for God's existence transforms *clear=true/untrue=unclear* into *being/nonbeing.*[7]

These transformations have a similarity to those employed in structural linguistics and anthropology. Lévi-Strauss' analysis of the mythology of North and South American Indians allows him to arrange his findings in structures based on oppositions of which "each is a function of all the others." Each pair of opposed terms *(male/female, sun/moon)* is capable of transformations of the kind found in Wölfflin *(painterly/linear=unclear/clear)* so that "potentially at least, the system is closed."[8] Without speculating on the appropriateness of applying these structures to non-Western cultures, and without insisting on the word structure in what follows, I want to suggest that when these binary oppositions are considered in all their implications—when they are considered for the full range of transformations of which they are capable—they reveal a vast, enclosed "architecture" of moral, religious and esthetic meanings.

Wölfflin's oppositions give a local version of this architecture. In its function as an enclosure, it finds an equally local metaphor for itself in the edges of the traditionally composed canvas. This metaphor is so fundamental to the meaning of Western painting that it is very seldom mentioned,[9] but it is implied in theories of compositional beauty, for composition must always place its elements in reference to the edge. When Pollock abandoned the enclosed, architectural space he naturally abandoned the traditional metaphor for it; that is, after he began his drip paintings Pollock no longer granted the edge its traditional value. This put him in a space—pictorial and cultural—where meaning is not in the elaboration of a pre-existing range of possibilities, but in the survival of individual intention

against the absence of those possibilities. Their absence is also the absence of the oppositional mode. In leaving architectural space, Pollock exchanged the painterly for the *painted*.

His first drip paintings didn't make it immediately clear that Wölfflin's "pairs of concepts" were no longer applicable. The paintings from 1947 to 1950 can be seen as extremes of linear abstraction. However, their "linearity" doesn't submit to the transformations which would place it—give it meaning—within the architectural space of traditional Western art and culture. Pollock's line has no representational or compositional intention so there are no external criteria by which to judge it clear or unclear. As for *open/closed* and *unity/multiplicity,* all four terms can be made to apply to these paintings—but none can be applied very convincingly. Nor does this "linearity" enforce a planar over a recessional reading of the paintings' space, which can be seen as chaotic, as a relief space built out slightly from the canvas, or a steady flow into an intricate mesh—as if

Mark Rothko: *Red-brown, Black, Green, Red,* 1962, 81 1/4 inches high. Marlborough gallery, New York.

Clyfford Still: *1964,* 1964, 9 feet high. Marlborough gallery.

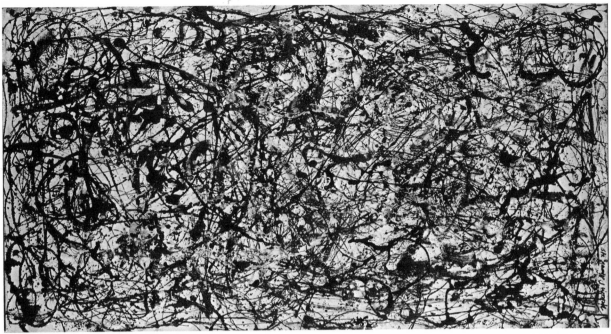

Jackson Pollock: *Painting* 1948, 47 7/8 inches high (coll. Mrs. Lee Krasner Pollock). Pollock, Rothko and Still were among postwar American abstractionists to abandon architectural space.

Morris Louis, in his *Unfurled* paintings, created a vast, edgeless expanse: *Beta Nu*, 1961, 102 inches high. Emmerich gallery, New York.

space were a fluid medium. In any case, there's no point in looking at these works as transformations of possibilities derived from the opposition *Renaissance/Baroque*.

If the earliest drip paintings are superficially linear, then the stained and poured black enamel on raw canvas paintings of 1951 and the heavily spattered pictures of 1952 are superficially painterly—but it's more accurate to say that with slight changes in paint consistency and gesture Pollock was able to produce works *painted* in a variety of ways.

Pollock's development after 1947 can be most easily described in the oppositional terms he left behind, but it would be a mistake to consider this development only from a formal point of view. As I suggested above, Wölfflin's oppositions are derived versions of more fundamental ones—*true/untrue, good/evil* and *clear/ unclear* in its rationalist sense. The inclusiveness of the

"space" defined by these oppositions insures that they are abstractions of social values: at their most ambiguous they become *individual/society* and *individual/ culture* (it's here that one could connect Wölfflin's oppositions to their source in Hegelian rationalism). In leaving the architectural space, Pollock escaped the ambiguities of its transformations, but in doing so he put himself in a space where the term *individual* finds no opposing term against which to define itself.

I have concentrated on Pollock because his work most readily invites and rejects the *painterly/linear* opposition, but he was not the only postwar American abstractionist to abandon the architectural space for an "incoherent," unstructured space. Mark Rothko, Clyfford Still and Barnett Newman produced paintings that don't depend for their meaning on traditional uses of material, composition or the edge. These painters are highly respected, but their influence has been limited, even where it has been claimed as fundamental. To reject the cultural space whose definition is founded in classical antiquity is an individual project. It not only doesn't attract followers, but, as we'll see below, doesn't permit them.

The classical space was rationalized in Renaissance perspective, a system which allows an enclosed space to radiate from fixed points along clearly defined lines. Previous linearity had defined figures and objects. The inventors of perspective gave these figures and objects a mathematically coherent pictorial architecture to inhabit. From ancient times until the present, standard theory has identified this coherence with beauty. However, *On the Sublime* (ca. 100 A.D.), the guide to rhetoric attributed to Longinus, suggests that great art is produced when this coherence is surpassed. Longinus provided arguments for the full range of esthetic opinion in eighteenth-century England. At one extreme, his notion of the exceptional work that culminates by transcending the rules upon which it is founded changes to a notion of individual genius which requires great art to be exceptional, unregulated and thoroughly individual, from its beginnings. This new theory of the

sublime suggests a cultural space in which the artist is isolated from a society which can provide no audience with a coherent set of values by which to judge his work.

A painter in the new sublime must invent his own values and, turning to formal matters, his own techniques. Faced with a blank canvas that has no stability to its edges and no potential for a traditional beauty, the painter often invents his own "tradition" from his new technique which of course cannot be contained within the traditional formulations *painterly/linear, open/closed* and so on. An eighteenth-century example can be seen in Alexander Cozens' *A New Method of Assisting the Invention in Drawing Original Compositions of Landscape* (1785). Cozens would begin his landscapes with a random blot of ink. No coherent composition results from this method, even where Cozens works his blots into representational landscapes. The meaning of works produced this way can be seen formally in their lack of containing edges and in their ability to do without traditional composition—Cozens called this "the uncommon spirit" of paintings begun with a blot, which "is not a drawing, but an assemblage of accidental shapes." In addition to their formal innovations, these

An earlier William Pettet, soft and inflected by faint glitterings: Untitled, 1968, 92 inches high. Museum of Modern Art. New York.

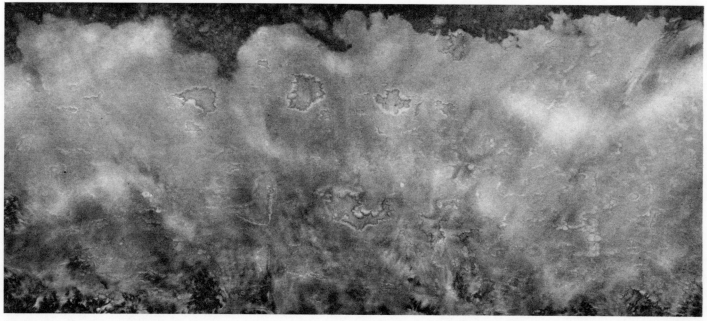

Pettet's later Baroque style, gesture in the service of composition:
Untitled, 1970, 75 1/2 inches high. Lannan Foundation collection, Palm Beach.

works provide the spectacle of an individual gesture which can find meaning only in its intensity—here a rather desperate reclamation of the representational—in the midst of a cultural space which is fundamentally unstructured.

For Longinus and others in the architectural space, "sublime" is a superlative, the word for the most elevated form of beauty. Outside that space it is not a term of approval. Formally, it designates a kind of pictorial space. More generally, it is the name of the cultural space inhabited by artists who have stepped outside the architecture defined by oppositions. One of the most important and most ambiguous of these oppositions is *audience/artist*. In abandoning the architectural space, the artist in the new sublime takes up the position of certain Romantics (Coleridge, Emerson) for whom the audience is not a well-defined set of cultivated people, but a vague, limitless presence, not necessarily human, and certainly not prepared by traditional education nor united by a shared sensibility.

The reaction to Pollock and other painters in the sublime was an attempt to reinstate traditional oppositions. The space defined by these oppositions is cultural before it is esthetic, and so it's not surprising that the first major reaction was not an art movement so much as a social movement, even a "sociology"—Pop Art. Its concerns were not the oppositions in the rarefied forms given to them by high culture, but a transformation of them which called into question high culture itself: *machine made=low culture/high culture=hand painted* where *hand painted* means *hand painted and nothing more* so that the transformation in this revised form is ironic—*low=good/bad=high*. This irony should not ob-

scure the fact that Pop Art was an attempt to return meaning, or "dimensionality," to the social space traditionally occupied by "the artist" and left uninhabited by Pollock and the others.

The formalist reaction to Pollock was an attempt to reinstate the critical apparatus from which the *painterly/linear* opposition derived. This development was given its most elaborate form in the writings of Clement Greenberg and Michael Fried. They were reactionary, not because they employed Wölfflin's terminology, which has persisted in American and English art criticism ever since Roger Fry introduced it in 1926,[10] but because they reached past Wölfflin to Aloïs Riegl for his opposition *optical/tactile*, a prior form of Wölfflin's "pairs of concepts." By concentrating on Pollock's stained-in paintings and following their influence on a limited number of artists (Helen Frankenthaler, Morris Louis, Kenneth Noland), the formalists attempted to make Pollock's career a source of the dialectical progression defined by—and defining—the architectural space. Their attempt required them to place Pollock's dripped and stained works at the optical pole in extreme opposition to Cubist, that is, tactile painting. This is a gross distortion.

In formalist usage, the illusionary space of abstract painting is called "optical" if the eye, upon entering it, enjoys a "purely optical experience as against optical experience modified or revised by tactile associations."[11] This formulation fails to account for the experience of Pollock's painting. As one's eye enters his illusionary space, one enters into—reconstructs in imagination—the gesture with which he produced it. This gesture is obviously tactile (it would be better to say athletic), but it is optical as well—this space requires of the eye an active, non-contemplative engagement. It's not that visual and physical gesture—the optical and the tactile—are joined here. It's that Pollock's paintings arrive from a gestural unity prior to the opposition, or even the distinction, between tactile and optical. The eye, upon entering this space, is in inextricable—synesthetic[12]—conjunction with the rest of the body. This entry is not a personal inflection of a pre-existing structure—the architecture of the painting or of the culture which presents the painting with its possibilities. It is an attempt to match the intensity of Pollock's original gesture, that is, to find in a consciousness of its own isolation and contingency an intensity able to withstand the incoherence of the space from which it arrives. (This space is cultural for Pollock, cultural and pictorial for the viewer.)

The formalists elaborated their notion of the "opti-cal" throughout the 1960s. They were joined by the anti-formalists, who inspired further transformations of the pairs of concepts originating with Wölfflin and Riegl. *Formal/anti-formal* became *decorative/non-decorative, illusionary/non-illusionary,* and so on.[13] These are interesting as examples of the reluctance to give up the assurances provided by the stability of the architectural space. A desperate form of this reluctance is found in Conceptual Art, which tries to hypostatize the traditional oppositions in concrete "art propositions."[14]

Pollock died in 1956; Rothko, Newman and Still continued to paint in the sublime space. Morris Louis entered it occasionally. His *Unfurled* paintings (1960-61), with their ribbons of color, create vast, edgeless space which cannot be enclosed within the *painterly/linear* opposition. Larry Poons's grid paintings

Painterly abstraction retaining architectural space:
Stephen Mueller's *Sky Blue Jeans,* 1969, 6 feet high.

Stephen Mueller: *China*, 1970, 80 inches
high. Feigen gallery, New York & Chicago.

(1961-68) are superficially architectural (Cubist), but
they are edgeless as well. Their flickering patterns of
dots are contained by the edge of the canvas, but only
in a literal—contingent—way, not structurally, for these
paintings are not compositional and therefore do not
contain within themselves any meaningful limits: according to their own "logic" they could be extended
forever.

However, both Poons and Louis were assimilated by
formalist analyses: their staining methods left the canvas
free of gesture and this made it easy to assume that their
space was open only to the eye, that Louis especially
was guiding abstraction, well within the architecture of
oppositions, toward an ideal of "purely optical experience" by reducing his concern to what is "unique to the
nature of [the] medium."[15] We've seen, in looking at
Pollock's drip paintings, that this reduction is mislead-

ing: perception is a synesthetic gesture from which an
optical component cannot be extracted. This is as true
of one's experience of paintings within the architectural
space as it is of those in the sublime space. The
difference is that in the sublime space the unity of
perception is taken into account in the course of a
concern with individual meaning; it is not obscured by a
transcendentalizing concern which makes art an attempt
to place the individual (artist or viewer) in a definitive
manner somewhere within a stable and pre-existing
cultural space.

If this unity—and inexhaustible richness—is only
implied in Poons's stained-in grid paintings, it was made
explicit in his *Night Journey* and other works of
1968-69. Here Poons gave up a stained-in flatness for
the deep space of the sublime. Depth appeared with his
acceptance of high-value contrast and in a vaguely

representational content—flurries of shape that hint at vast stretches of geography or sky. Sometimes the containing function of the edge is recalled, as when Poons divides the canvas more or less evenly with a vertical line, but the two "halves" rarely serve each other in establishing compositional balance. Poons refers to the edge of the canvas in order to suggest that it no longer has even the faint containing power that subsisted in his grids against their endlessness. With these heavily inflected paintings, Poons completely rejected the architectural space, or—to use the terms in which these problems offered themselves in the 1960s—he was no longer placing himself according to the oppositions *optical/tactile* or *Impressionist/Cubist*.

This rejection is continued in Poons's series of heavily poured and caked paintings, first shown in 1969, but it is much more conscious in the paintings of Gary Bower and John Torreano. Each in his own way establishes a pattern—a grid or scattering of dots—then dissolves it in washes and overlays of color which open onto the sublime, edgeless space. Their patterns (which have recently faded somewhat, especially in Torreano's work) only refer to Cubism; they are not linear in the traditional sense for they are not dissolved by the painterly—they're dissolved by the *painted*. Structure is painted away or intensely localized in a gesture whose meaning is that it belongs to an individual who refuses to be guided by a pre-existing architecture of meanings—one who, even after he invents an architecture of his own (a contingent pattern), is guided only by a consciousness

A David Diao wide-scrape painting stretched or disjointed by division: *1971-A*, 1971, 90 1/2 inches high. Paula Cooper gallery, New York.

In the isolation and reflexivity of painting in the sublime space, a new kind of gesture is another beginning:
David Diao's single wide-scrape painting (untitled), 1971, 68 inches high. Dunkelman gallery, Toronto.

of his isolation in the sublime. His art is in turning this consciousness into a gesture effective against that isolation—for the sublime usually obliterates those who enter it.

The paintings of Bower and Torreano are fully achieved though, to a superficial view, they might seem to occupy transitional positions in a development from compositional to sublime painting. This would be to impose a notion of coherent historical progress in a space that does not permit it. As soon as one leaves the architectural space with its dialectic of elaborations and transformations, one leaves as well its orderly flow of time. The possibilities for painting are not functions of each other in the sublime space and likewise painters there cannot be arranged in such oppositions as *Poussin/Rubens, Ingres/Delacroix, Symbolist/Neo-Impressionist, Constructivist/Surrealist,* etc. Influence can be only vaguely traced in the sublime because it is not coherent enough to permit a clear advance from one position to another. (A painter, say a "Lyrical Abstractionist," who imitates Pollock, does not thereby enter the sublime; he takes up a position in the architecture of oppositions defined in advance by formalist criticism of the '60s.)

The painter who has left the architectural space has only a tangential, ambiguous relationship to other painters who have done the same. This point can be made specific with a look at David Diao's painting. For several years Diao painted monochrome or two-color works whose stained-in paint is inflected by elegant scrapings. This creates an interest in the play of reflective against non-reflective surfaces. But rather than "against" one should say "in the vicinity of": these paintings are without composition—they are edgeless; they provide no framework within which a clear opposition can define itself. But if the surface will not be resolved into the opposition *reflective/non-reflective,* then there can be no opposition *surface/depth.* The depths of these paintings remain inexhaustibly ambiguous, as can be seen by comparing them to the depths in "similar" paintings.

William Pettet's early works are soft, inflected only by faint unanticipated glitterings. In their context, Diao's scraped inflections seem very strong; they draw the depths of the painting "toward" them—the painting grows shallow. In the context of Ronnie Landfield's painting, Diao's depths reassert themselves; Landfield's high-keyed suppression, but not absence of, value contrast gives Diao's monochrome a slow, retreating

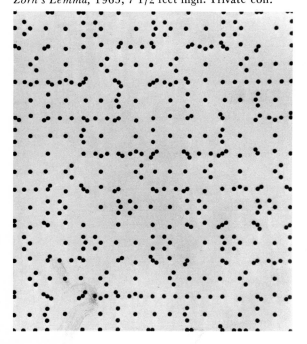

Early Poons, contained but structurally boundless: *Zorn's Lemma,* 1963, 7 1/2 feet high. Private coll.

Depth elicited by vague representational content: Larry Poons, untitled, 1968, 8 1/2 feet high. Woodward Foundation, Washington, D.C.

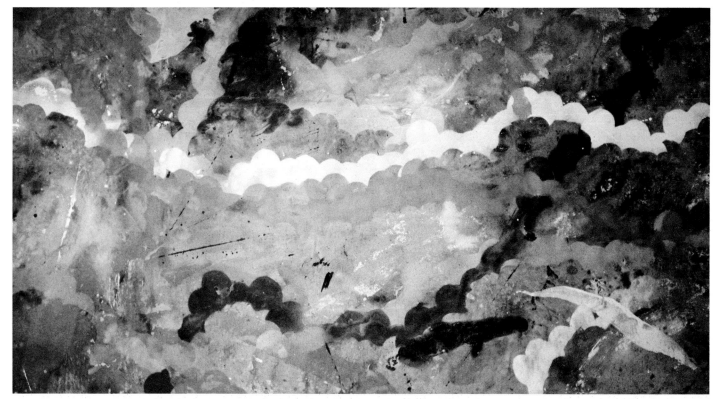

A unifying intensity in gesture vs. potential chaos in methods:
John Seery's *Mingus*, 1970, 9 1/2 feet high. Emmerich gallery.

motion. One is carried "toward" the monochrome itself—toward this aspect of Diao's painting. This motion is speeded up in the context provided by John Seery's intricate, fully occupied depths.

In the sublime, one's own development becomes a source of unresolvable ambiguity. Diao has recently exchanged his multitude of small, elegant inflections for one wide scrape over a canvas prepared with layers of

Architectural space rejected in heavily poured and caked work:
Poons's *Dangerous B*, 1969. Coll. Richard Weisman, New York.

color. These new works, especially the ones divided into two equal parts, show that Diao's sublime, like Barnett Newman's, is not an evasion of the edges of the canvas. Rather, it is a way of filling the canvas so that its literal shape is—to use Newman's word—"busted." This busting the shape of the canvas is a defeat for traditional structure. It is often quite violent with Newman, more a case of stretching or disjointing in Diao's recent work.

Far from clarifying his earlier works (as, for example, Synthetic Cubism helped to clarify Analytic Cubism), Diao's new paintings render them more ambiguous. His single gesture is both more and less unified—both more and less random—than his earlier multiple gestures. There is a superficial resemblance between the two ways of inflecting the surface—they are both scrapings—but they are not transformations of each other. There is intensity in the new inflection because it is not derived; it doesn't refer to a model of (dialectical) progress already established—it's not a continuation, it's a beginning. The individual's success against the contingency and incoherence of the sublime space is in a reflexiveness which turns the individual's share of that contingency back upon himself in the form of self-consciousness. For this to be a full share of contingency, each gesture must be a beginning.

The intensity required for this project can be seen in the relentless variousness of John Seery's methods. He scrapes, sprays, stains his canvases. Recently he has put them underwater to soak until the paint reveals itself in ways not available to more direct "gestures." Just as Pollock's early drip paintings are not linear in relation to his later more heavily splashed ones—for the later ones

Intricate, fully occupied depths through varying methods of applying color: John Seery's *Payshtha*, 1970, 118 inches high. Art Institute of Chicago, on extended loan by the Richard Gray gallery.

are not painterly in the traditional sense—so Seery's scraping is not a transformation of his staining technique, nor is his staining a transformation of his spraying. Above all, he does not soak his canvases in order to soften the differences between his various techniques. It is not a "dialectical" process intended to unify opposing results. In fact it accentuates their differences, carrying his works beyond the space where differences can be contained in coherent oppositions.

Seery's methods are brought together to undercut each other—to impinge, sometimes chaotically, upon each other. The unity that results is not between methods, textures or shapes and colors composed according to a pre-existing ideal to which composition refers by transcending its own particularity in an individual painting. The unity here defies the medium in which it persists, for it is the unifying (immanent) intensity of Seery's gesture—his intention *to paint*. His success, especially in his most recent, most violent paintings, is in making this intention survive against the potential for chaos in his methods, and in his tendency to make use of all of these methods in a single work.

The striations in Larry Poons's heavily poured paintings invoke the canvas edge, but the edge is without containing power: *569*, 1969, 115 inches high. David Mirvish gallery, Toronto.

Cubist grid dissolved by the painted:
Gary Bower's *Rearview*, 1971, 5 feet high.

To enter the sublime space is to give up the assurances offered by the architecture of values derived from antiquity and the Renaissance. This is not just a way of being original. It's a dangerous undertaking, the project of an individuality which can never be fully "appreciated" because its isolation in its own unity—its reflexiveness—doesn't permit full critical comment, unlike a career guided by the structure of the architectural space, part of the elaboration of which is a long-standing and self-justifying critical tradition.

Because of its dangers—Edmund Burke insisted longest on its terrors—many young artists who recently began to enter the sublime have now, one or two years later, retreated from it. The "Lyrical Abstraction" show at the Larry Aldrich Museum in the spring of 1970 (and again at the Whitney Museum, spring, 1971) was filled with works by painters who had taken up tentative positions toward the sublime. But the sublime obliterates tentativeness. Most of the works on view in these exhibitions failed to show any individual intention whatsoever.

In a few cases this tentativeness manages to maintain itself in an uneasy eclecticism. Recently, Landfield has imposed a structure of stripes in solid colors on the chaotically stained-in areas of his canvas. This puts his work under the influence of composition without really composing them. They now take their interest from a vague elaboration of the opposition *painterly/linear*.

Pattern fades into sublime, edgeless space: John Torreano, untitled, 1971, 112 1/2 inches high. Reese Palley gallery.

An impulse toward the sublime in fundamentally painterly work: Philip Wofford's *Revelation's Abyssal Blue*, 1970, 9 feet high.

Stripe structure evokes the opposition painterly/linear: Ronnie Landfield's *Storm Thread*, 1971, 9 feet high. David Whitney gallery.

This is an attempt to make up in traditional references—and assurances—for a lack of the intensity which would allow these paintings to survive in the sublime space toward which Landfield's work was heading at the time of the first "Lyrical Abstraction" show. Since the sublime doesn't grant any value to traditional progressions, perhaps this very *heading toward* prevented Landfield from arriving.

Much the same can be said about Pettet's recent, heavily gestural but at the same time very obviously composed—even Baroque—paintings. Gesture in the service of composition produces the painterly, not the *painted,* as with Philip Wofford's paintings, which for all their energy and textural variation—all their yearning for the sublime—are held back by edges as fundamentally Cubist in their effect as those in the works of Stephen Mueller, a young painterly painter who never indulged in the ploy of seeming to reject the architectural space.

Pop Art, formalism and anti-formalism were attempts to reinstate the architecture of oppositions. Perhaps this recent use of the look of sublime painting is another such attempt. Its function would be to revive the opposition *painterly=Action-Painting/Hard-Edge Painting=linear* which was obscured for a time by formalist insistence on the opposition *optical/tactile.*

The difference between the two sorts of painting we've considered here is that one transcends itself toward the pre-existing values from which it takes its possibilities, while the meaning of the other is immanent in each painting—as it is produced or as it is viewed. But the architecture of values which defines Western composition and pictorial beauty has been examined endlessly by modern painters, most intensely during the Cubist experiments, repetitiously and to less and less effect in the Conceptualist "investigations." It's not surprising then that our discussion of the meaning of painting in the sublime allows us to see past the repetitious transcendentalizing in the architectural space to its own version of immanent meaning.

For example, Robert Ryman's painting does not *refer* to the generalized Western (for a modern painter, Cubist) architecture of values. Thanks to their "blankness," to the eccentric, intensely localized and individual way they impose on their regularized formats, and to their ability to engage the peculiarities of their urban surroundings, they *inhabit* their architecture, without engaging its traditional oppositions—without transcendentalizing. Ryman's brushwork can be heavy, energetic, even messy, but his paintings are not painterly, rather—like certain of Willem de Kooning's very different, but equally individual and equally unsublime paintings—they are *painted*.

1. Heinrich Wölfflin, *Principles of Art History* (1915), New York, 1950, p. 14.
2. *Ibid*,. pp. 14-16.
3. *Ibid.*, p. 227.
4. Francis V. O'Conner, *Jackson Pollock*, Museum of Modern Art., New York, 1967, from an interview taped in the summer of 1950, p. 79.
5. Wölfflin, op. cit., pp. 14-16.
6. Descartes, *The Principles of Philosophy* (1644), *Philosophical Works*, translated by Haldane. Vol. 1, London, 1911, 237 ff.
7. Descartes, *Meditations on First Philosophy* (1641), *Philosophical Works*, Vol. 1. London, 1911, 157 ff.
8. Claude Lévi-Strauss, "The Sex of the Heavenly Bodies," *Introduction to Structuralism*, ed. Michael Lane, New York, 1970, p. 337.
9. A notable exception to this oversight is: Meyer Schapiro, "On Some Problems in the Semiotics of Visual Art: Field and Vehicle in Image-Signs," *Semiotica*, Paris, I, iii, 1969.
10. Roger Fry, "The Seicento" (1926), *Transformations*, New York, 1956, 127 ff.
11. Clement Greenberg, "Modernist Painting," *Art and Literature*, Spring, 1965; see also Michael Fried, *Three American Painters*, Cambridge, 1965, p. 14.
12. Maurice Merleau-Ponty, *The Phenomenology of Perception* (1945), London, 1962, 228 ff.
13. Robert Morris, "Antiform," *Artforum*, April, 1968; "Notes on Sculpture, Part 4: Beyond Objects," *Artforum*, April 1969; "The Art of Existence," *Artforum*, January, 1971; James Monte and Marcia Tucker, *Anti-Illusion: Procedure/Materials*, Whitney Museum, New York, 1969.
14. Joseph Kosuth, "Art after Philosophy," *Conceptual Art and Conceptual Aspects*, New York Cultural Center, 1970, p. 4.
15. Clement Greenberg, op. cit. p. 102.

Landfield's earlier heading toward sublime space: *Off the Coast*, 1969, 8 feet high. Lannan Foundation collection.

Philip Wofford: *The Tides*, 1969, 8 feet high. David Whitney gallery, New York.

Index of Illustrations

Page numbers in italics indicate colorplates

Bassano, Jacopo   *Head of an Apostle*, 51
Boldini, Giovanni   *Mme. Marthe Letellier*, 16
Boucher, François   *A Summer Pastoral*, 80
Bower, Gary   *Rearview*, 144
Brueghel, Jan the Elder   *Dogs*, 73
  Donkeys, Monkeys and Other Animals, 72
Canaletto, Antonio   *The Doge and Officials Visiting the Scuola San Rocco*, detail, 40
  The Old Fish Market, 54
Carpaccio, Vittore   *The Dream of St. Ursula*, 42
  The Reception of the English Ambassadors, 42
Cézanne, Paul   *The Small Bridge*, 95
Claude Lorrain   *Landscape with Mercury and the Shepherd Battus*, 92
Constable, John   *The Cenotaph*, 100
  Cirrus Clouds, 98
  Dedham Mill, 97
  Dedham Vale Seen from a Wooded Hill, 97
  The Hay Wain, detail, 90
  The Leaping Horse, 94
  The Lock, 95
  On the Stour, 100
  Salisbury Cathedral from the Bishop's Garden, 102, 103
  Salisbury Cathedral from the River, 102
  View of the Stour near Dedham, 101
  View on the Stour, Dedham Church in the Distance, 96
  Waterloo Bridge, 100
  Weymouth Bay, 1816, 98
  Weymouth Bay, 1820, 99
Cozens, John Robert   *Florence from near the Cascine*, 93
Crome, John   *The Beaters*, 93
Diao, David   *1971-A*, 138
  Untitled, 1971, *139*
Fragonard, Jean-Honoré   *Abbé de Saint-Non in Spanish Costume*, 78
  Blindman's Buff, 80
  The Consequences of War, 81
  Fountain of Love, 86
  The Holy Family with Angels, after Rembrandt, 81
  The Lady Gardener, 85
  The Musical Contest, 80
  The New Model, 82
  Portrait of M. de la Bretèche, 78
  St. Jerome Reading, 85
  The Schoolmistress, 84
  Self-Portrait, 87
  Shepherd in a Landscape, 84
  The Stolen Kiss, 87
  The Stolen Shift, 83
  The Swing, detail, 85
  The Warrior, 79
  The Watering-place, 84
  A Young Scholar, 76
Gainsborough, Thomas   *The Fallen Tree*, 93
Giorgione   *Old Man's Head*, 44
  The Three Philosophers, detail, 44
Guardi, Francesco   *The Grand Canal at the Pescheria, Venice*, 46, 47
  The Grand Canal Looking toward S. Stae, 54
  Piazza San Marco during the Sensa Fair, 54
Guardi, Giovanni Antonio   *Aurora*, details, 55
Hofmann, Hans   *Bedeutungsvolles Ahnen*, 112
  Birdcage – Variation 2, *111*
  Exuberance, 110
  Flaming Lava, 114
  The Garden, 110
  Joy Sparks of The Gods, 106
  Little Cherry (Renate Series No. 1), 113
  Magnum Opus, 112
  The Scorpion, 113
  Untitled, 1936, 108
Kooning, Willem de   *Beach Scene*, 124
  Big, 124
  Clam Digger, 122
  Figure at Gerard Beach, 122
  Japanese Village, 125
  Landing Place, 121
  Landscape at Stanton Street, 126
  Love to Wakako, 121
  The Marshes, 124
  Minnie Mouse, 127
  Mother and Child, 123
  Photograph of the artist, 120
  Reflections – to Kermit for Our Trip to Japan, 121
  Sting Ray, 126
  Table and Chair, 125
  Valentine, 122
  Woman with Corset and Long Hair, 124
  Weekend at Mr. and Mrs. Krisher, 118
  Woman in Amagansett, 123
Landfield, Ronnie   *Off the Coast*, 147
  Storm Thread, 146
Longhi, Pietro   *Lady and Gentleman on a Divan*, 53
  The Morning Cup of Chocolate, detail, 53
Louis, Morris   *Beta Nu*, 133
Maffei, Francesco   *The Assumption*, detail, 51
  Mme. Jean Martin in Black Hat, 16
Michelangelo   *Bearded Slave*, 21

Monet, Claude   *Nymphéas*, 15
  Portrait of Jean Monet, 15
Mueller, Stephen   *China*, 137
  Sky Blue Jeans, 136
Pellegrini, Giovanni Antonio   *Europe*, 53
  Venus and Cupid, 53
Pettet, William   Untitled, 1968, 134
  Untitled, 1970, 135
Pollock, Jackson   *Number 1, 1950 (Lavender Mist)*, 17
  Painting, 133
Poons, Larry   *Dangerous B*, 141
  569, *143*
  Untitled, 1968, 140
  Zorn's Lemma, 140
Rembrandt van Rijn   *Christ between Two Thieves*, 69
  Christ Healing the Sick, 71
  Christ Presented to the People, 64
  Christ Speaking to His Disciples, 71
  The Concord of State, 68
  The Holy Family with Angels, 81
  Joseph Telling His Dreams, 70, 71
  Lamentation over the Dead Christ, 69
  Portrait of the Jewish Physician Ephraim Bueno, 65
  St. John the Baptist Preaching, 68; detail 58
Renoir, Auguste   *Sunset at Sea*, 14
Rodin, Pierre-Auguste   *Balzac*, 21
Roman painting   *Homeric House*, 33
  House of the Griffins, 28
  House of Livia, 33
  House of the Vettii, 34, 37
  Ulysses and the Lestrygonians, 31
  Villa of Agrippa Postumus, 35
  Villa Boscoreale, 29, 30
  Villa Farnesina, 36
  Villa of Mysteries, 26
  Villa Publius Sinistor, 29
Roman sculpture   *Ara Pacis*, detail, 32
Rothko, Mark   *Red-brown, Black, Green, Red*, 132
Rubens, Peter Paul   *Adoration of the Magi*, 66
  Christ Carrying the Cross, 62
  The Consequences of War, 81
  The Flight of St. Barbara, 60, 61
  The Garden of Love, detail, 13
  Lyricorum Libri, 63
  The Meeting of Abraham and Melchisedech, 67
  Negro Head, 73
  Study of a Head, 66
Ruysdael, Salomon van   *A River Scene with Cattle*, 92
Ryman, Robert   Untitled, 1970, 130
Seery, John   *Mingus*, 141
  Payshtha, *142*
Still, Clyfford   *1964*, 132
Tiepolo, Giovanni Battista   *Africa*, detail, 49
  Crowning with Thorns, detail, 49
  The Triumph of Venus, 50
  Virgin and Child with St. Joseph, 48
Tintoretto, Jacopo   *The Last Supper*, detail, 52
Titian   *The Annunciation*, detail, 48
  Man on Horseback and Fallen Warrior, 48
  Man with a Glove, detail, 45
  The Rape of Europa, detail, cover
  Young Lady as Venus Binding the Eyes of Cupid, 22
Torreano, John   Untitled, 1971, 145
Turner, Joseph Mallord William   *A Frosty Morning Sunrise*, 94
Velázquez   *The Infanta Maria Theresa*, detail, 10
  Las Meninas, detail, 18
  Philip IV of Spain in Brown and Silver, detail, 4
  Portrait of the Count-Duke of Olivares, 23
  Portrait of Philip IV, 12
Venetian, mosaic   *The Flood*, detail, 42
Veronese, Paolo   *Baptism and Temptation of Christ*, detail, 43
Wofford, Philip   *Revelation's Abyssal Blue*, 146
  The Tides, 147

Credits

Cover: Isabella Stewart Gardner Museum, Boston. Colorplates on pp. 43, 46-47, 50, 70, 99: from Mondadori, Verona. 67: National Gallery, Washington, D.C. 79: Clark Art Institute, Williamstown, Mass. 102: National Gallery, London. 111, 114: Emmerich Gallery, New York. 139: Cole Color Prints, Danbury, Conn. 142: Richard Grey Gallery, Chicago. 143: David Mirvish Gallery, Toronto. 146: David Whitney Gallery, New York. Photographs on pp. 28, 29, 34, 35: German Archaeological Inst., Rome. 32, 37: Anderson, Rome. 40: National Gallery, London. Mas, Barcelona. 95: Tooth Gallery, London (1950). 97: Christie's, London (1959). 98: Victoria & Albert Museum, London. 102, 103: Frick Collection, New York. 112: Emmerich Gallery, New York. 136: Feigen Gallery, New York. 140: Graham Gund, Cambridge, Mass. Other reprod., pp. 29, 33: L. Curtius, *Die Wandmalerei Pompejis* (G. Olms, Hildesheim, 1960). 33: K. Schefold, *Vergessenes Pompeji* (Francke Verlag, Bern, 1962).

M. KNOEDLER & CO

Old Masters • Impressionists • American Art • Modern Masters

LOUISE BOURGEOIS

SALVADOR DALI

WILLEM DE KOONING

DUCHAMP-VILLON

ARSHILE GORKY

ETIENNE HAJDU

EVA HESSE

VASSILY KANDINSKY

BERTO LARDERA

HENRY MOORE

ERNST WILHELM NAY

BARNETT NEWMAN

EMIL NOLDE

FAIRFIELD PORTER

MAURICE PRENDERGAST

BERNARD ROSENTHAL

TONY SMITH

PIERRE SOULAGES

BRAM VAN VELDE

VIEIRA DA SILVA

PAUL WALDMAN

Cable address "Knoedler" NEW YORK, 21 East 70th Street
PARIS, 85bis Faubourg St. Honoré • LONDON, 34 St. James's Street

Why Collectors Collect Our Catalogs

Because, for the serious collector, PB catalogues are a prerequisite to the pursuit of fine art and antiques. Considering that over three-fourths of all auction sales of fine art and antiques in the U.S. are conducted by Parke-Bernet Galleries, one can readily understand why the key to this marketplace—the catalogue—is an indispensable guide for all collectors. Beautiful and enduring, Parke-Bernet catalogues are the culmination of diligent research by the Galleries' experts. Together with post-sale price lists, they keep you *au courant* with your field of interest.

Published in fifteen categories from antiquities to modern paintings and sculpture, these sourcebooks give you a reference library of unequalled excellence. Write for a subscription form. If you also indicate your field or fields of interest—paintings (traditional or modern), prints, sculpture, furniture and decorative arts, Oriental art, antiquities, or silver, we will send you a sample catalogue at no charge.

Address Catalogue Department ANA
Parke-Bernet Galleries, Inc.
980 Madison Avenue, New York 10021

Parke-Bernet

Allan Stone Gallery
48 East 86th St.

Willem De Kooning 1949

Oct.

Willem De Kooning
40's - 50's

Nov.

James Grashow
"Murder Maché"

Dec.

Nancy Drosd
"The Party"

BOSTON...
is an Art Center

- ■ faculty of professional artists
- ■ bachelor's and master's degrees
- ■ painting ■ sculpture
- ■ art education
- ■ advertising design
- ■ interior design
- ■ summer programs at Tanglewood

BOSTON UNIVERSITY

School of Fine and Applied Arts
855 Commonwealth Avenue
Boston, Mass. 02215

The European Collection includes:

BERNARD
BONNARD
BOUDIN
BOURDELLE
BRAQUE
CHAGALL
COROT
COURBET
DEGAS
DERAIN
D'ESPAGNAT
DUFRESNE
DUFY
DUNOYER DE SEGONZAC
FORAIN
GAUGUIN
GUILLAUMIN
JONGKIND
LEBOURG

LEPINE
L'OISEAU
MATISSE
MODIGLIANI
MONET
MORISOT
PASCIN
PISSARRO
RENOIR
ROUAULT
ROUSSEAU, HENRI
SEVERINI
SIGNAC
SOUTINE
UTRILLO
VALLOTTON
VALTAT
VUILLARD

JOSÉ PACHECO
by Amadeo Modigliani
Oil on canvas
25½ x 21¼ inches
Signed lower left: Modigliani

The American Collection includes:

BLUEMNER
BURCHFIELD
CASSATT
CHURCH
COLE
COPLEY
CROPSEY
DURAND
EAKINS
EARL
FRIESEKE
GLACKENS
HARTLEY
HASSAM
HAWTHORNE

HEADE
HENRI
HOMER
JOHNSON
KENSETT
MARIN
MAURER
MORAN
PRENDERGAST
ROBINSON
SARGENT
SLOAN
SULLY
WEST
YATES

MRS. JOSHUA WINSLOW
by John Singleton Copley
Pastel on paper
22½ x 17½ inches

Hirschl & Adler Galleries inc.

21 East 67th Street New York 10021   (212) 535-8810   Tuesdays-Fridays: 9:30 to 5:30, Saturdays: 9:30 to 5

153

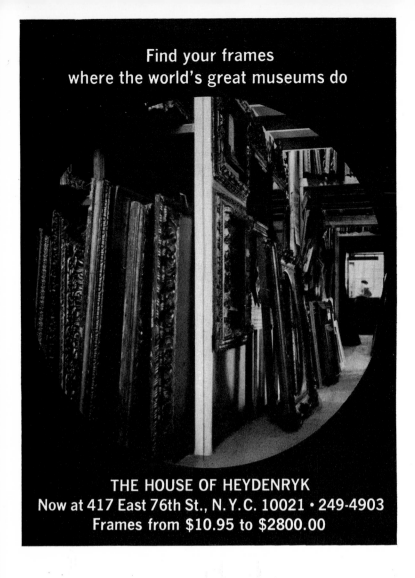

New AND Exciting

ARTBOOKS FROM **ABRAMS**

EDWARD HOPPER *with text by Lloyd Goodrich.* 226 illustrations, with 81 extra-large in full color. 272 pages, 16 x 13".
Price through December 31, 1971: $42.50. Thereafter $50.00

EYEWITNESS TO SPACE *by Hereward Lester Cooke, with the collaboration of James D. Dean; foreword by J. Carter Brown; preface by Thomas O. Paine.* 258 illustrations, including 113 huge plates in full color. 241 pages, 16 x 14".
Price through December 31, 1971: $30.00. Thereafter $35.00

AMERICAN INDIAN ART *text by Norman Feder.* 302 illustrations, including 60 large hand-tipped plates in full color. 448 pages, 11⅜ x 10⅝".
Price through December 31, 1971: $30.00. Thereafter $35.00

THE MOST EXTRAORDINARY GIFT BOOK OF 1970 IS NOW AVAILABLE AGAIN!

NORMAN ROCKWELL Artist and Illustrator *by Thomas S. Buechner.* This large, colorful and beautifully bound book includes all the wonderful Rockwell paintings America has known and loved for more than 60 years. 614 illustrations, including 127 pages in large full color. 328 pages. 12¼ x 17". $60.00

MICHELANGELO: The Complete Paintings, Sculpture and Drawings *by Frederick Hartt.* 1,033 illustrations. 876 pages. 3 volumes boxed. 9¾ x 13". $50.00

MAX ERNST: Histoire Naturelle. *Preface by Jean Arp.* 23 facsimile lithographs in a special portfolio. 12¾ x 19½". $50.00

PABLO PICASSO: *Le Gout Du Bonheur.* 68 drawings. 9⅞ x 12⅜". Boxed.
Price through December 31, 1971: $400.00. Thereafter $500.00

ENCYCLOPEDIA OF THEMES AND SUBJECTS IN PAINTING *by Howard Daniel, introduction by John Berger.* 332 illustrations including 32 in full color. 252 pages, 5⅞ x 8¼". $7.50

THE BEGINNING OF THE BEGINNING *by Joseph James Akston, introduction by James A. Michener, commentary by Gordon Brown.* Twelve hand-tipped plates in full color. 64 pages, 10¼ x 14". $15.00

THE SISTINE CHAPEL *by Roberto Salvini, Rittore Camesasca and C. L. Ragghianti.* Two volumes with 269 hand-tipped color plates and three- and four-page foldouts. 12¾ x 15⅞". Slipcased. $275.00

GEORGES BRAQUE *Texts by Francis Ponge and Pierre Descargues, foreword by André Malraux.* 152 illustrations, including 86 in full color. 230 pages, 11 x 11¾".
Price through December 31, 1971: $40.00. Thereafter $45.00

DALI BY DALI 80 illustrations, including 60 in full color. 160 pages, 5¼ x 7½". $7.95

VICTOR VASARELY *by Werner Spies,* 202 illustrations, including 74 in full color. 214 pages, 11 x 11¾".
Price through December 31, 1971: $35.00. Thereafter $40.00

THE TAMARIND BOOK OF LITHOGRAPHY: Art & Technique *by Garo Z. Antreasian and Clinton Adams,* 479 illustrations, including 87 in full color. 474 pages, 8¾ x 11½". $25.00

OCEANIC ART: Myth, Man and Image in the South Seas *by Carl A. Schmitz.* 337 illustrations, including 50 hand-tipped plates in full color, plus 6 maps. 420 pages, 9¾ x 11¼".
Price through December 31, 1971: $30.00. Thereafter $35.00

THE LAW AND THE PROPHETS *based on the NBC Project 20 program by Richard Hanser and Donald B. Hyatt.* 195 illustrations with 173 in full color. 356 pages, 9 x 11½".
Price through December 31, 1971: $22.50. Thereafter $25.00

ROY LICHTENSTEIN *by Diane Waldman.* 183 illustrations, including 85 hand-tipped plates in full color. 242 pages, 12⅜ x 12". $25.00

HUSAIN *Texts by Richard Bartholomew and Shiv S. Kapur.* 192 illustrations, including 53 hand-tipped plates in full color. 242 pages, 12⅜ x 12". $25.00

HARRY N. ABRAMS, INC.
TIMES MIRROR

110 EAST 59TH STREET, NEW YORK, N.Y. 10022

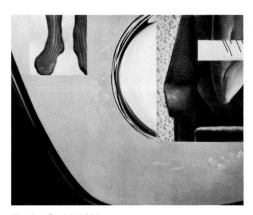

158

Spencer A. Samuels & Company, Ltd.

18 East 76, New York
By appointment:
YUkon 8-4556

Master Paintings,
Drawings and Sculpture
from the Fourteenth
to the Twentieth Century

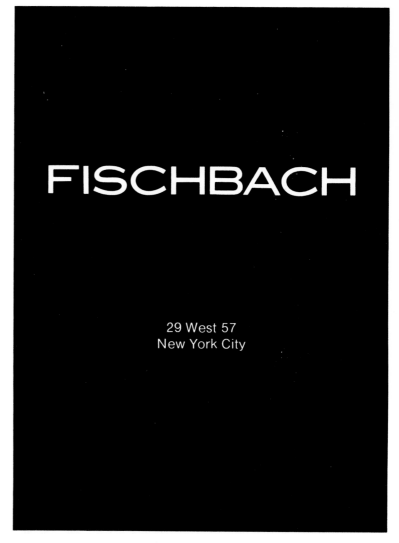

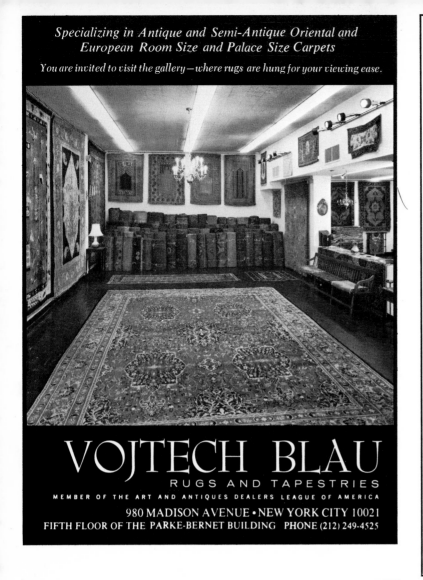